"A remarkable book that breathes new life into explorations of what constitutes "femininity." Hillel's vision of women's sexuality is new, timely, provocative and of crucial importance for everyone. Her approach is both earthy and spiritual and utterly dispels once and for all any idea that Jungian psychology has nothing significant to say about the instincts."

—ANDREW SAMUELS
Author of *The Political Psyche* and *Jung and Post-Jungians*

———

"I re-read your manuscript last night after we spoke and I will say again . . . It is wonderful! Clear and flowing and very moving. It is as if I am visiting with you. You write with so much compassion and understanding. It is as if you have had the experiences yourself and the reader's hearts are touched and our feelings are evoked for this book speaks to our souls. Thank you!"

—AURORA TERRENUS
Author of *The Shroud of Sophia*

THE REDEMPTION OF THE
FEMININE EROTIC SOUL

On The Hudson

Jung

BOOK SERIES

The New York Center for Jungian Studies presents
conferences and seminars in the U.S. and abroad,
including its Jung On The Hudson seminars held
each summer in the historic Hudson Valley. The
N.Y. Center seminars, book series and continuing
education programs are designed for individuals
from all fields as well as mental health professionals
who are interested in exploring the relevance of
Jung's ideas to their personal lives and/or professional
activities. The Center offers individual, couple and
group counseling, and provides consulting services
and mediation for family businesses and corporations.

For more information, please contact:
The New York Center for Jungian Studies
121 Madison Avenue, New York, NY 10016
Telephone: 212-689-8238 or Fax: 212-889-7634

The REDEMPTION
of the FEMININE
EROTIC SOUL

*Over the entrance to the sanctuary of Asklepios Temple in Epidaurus
(the Greek God of Healing) are images of Eros and Methe:
Love and Ecstasy as healing psychic powers.*

DR. RACHEL HILLEL

NICOLAS-HAYS, INC.
York Beach, Maine

First published in 1997 by
NICOLAS-HAYS, INC.
P. O. Box 612
York Beach, ME 03910-0612

Distributed to the trade by
SAMUEL WEISER, INC.
P. O. Box 612
York Beach, ME 03910-0612

03 02 01 00 99 98 97
9 8 7 6 5 4 3 2 1

Library of Congress Cataloging-in-Publication Data

Hillel, Rachel.
    The redemption of the feminine erotic soul / Rachel Hillel.
        p.   cm.
    Includes bibliographical reference and index.
    ISBN 0-89254-038-9 (paper : alk. paper)
    1. Psychotherapy—Erotic aspects. 2. Women—Psychology.
    3. Goddess religion. 4. Femininity. 5. Sex—Religious aspects.
    6. Jungian psychology. I. Title.
    RC489.E75H55   1997
    616.89'14'082—dc21   97-27481
                                                                CIP

Printed in the United States of America
BJ

Cover art is *The Source*, 1856 by Jean Auguste Dominique Ingres (1780-1867), Musee
d'Orsay, Paris/Bridgeman Art Library, London. Used by permission
GIRAUDON/BRIDGEMAN ART LIBRARY

Excerpts from "Ithaca," "Walls," "Return," "Understanding," and "Sensual Delight"
in *The Complete Poems of Cavafy*, copyright © 1961 and renewed 1987 by Rae Dalven.
Reprinted by kind permission of the Estate of C. P. Cavafy, Harcourt Brace &
Company, Orlando, and Hogarth Press, London.

*The paper used in this publication meets the minimum requirements
of the American National Standard for Permanence of Paper for
Printed Library Materials Z39.48-1984.*

For my children
Adi, Ron, Sari, Ori, Shira
Much love from your Eama

Table of Contents

Foreword BY ALICE JOHNSTON xi
Introduction BY NANCY QUALLS-CORBETT xiii
Acknowledgments xvii
Reflections xix

Prologue: The Inborn Religious Instinct:
Confessing an Early Experience of the Goddess, 1

Chapter 1: An Awakening into the Modern Feminine Quandary, 7

Dream: Jung and the Vulva 9
Dream: Healing the Wounded Vulva 15
Big Dreams: For Whom Are They Dreamed? 21
De Profundis: The Purpose of the Work 25

Chapter 2: Homeward: An Inauguration into
Feminine Sensuality—The Goddess' Veiled Reality, 33

Epiphany: The Showing Forth 35
The Gazebo: Vistas from an Enchanted Pavilion 37
Another Goddess Worshipper 39
A Tormented Hero 41
Ambivalence: A Restrained Redemption
  of Feminine Erotic Sensuality 46
Dawn 53

Chapter 3: Unbound from the Past, 55

Gleaning: Is Anyone There? 57
What Ails My Women Analysands:
    The Loss of the Goddess' Sacred Vulva 63
Regaining the Goddess' Sacred Vulva
    through Dreamwork 67

*Chapter 4: The Restoration of the Feminine
within Monotheism, 77*

The Massadah Dream: Diagnosis of Feminine Collective
    Suicide 79
Safed Dream: Prognosis of Contemporary Deliverance 84
Massadah and Safed Dreams .91
Active Imagination: An Autonomous Rejection by the
    Unconscious—A Dialogue Between a Modern Feminine
    Ego and an Arab Woman .93

*Chapter 5: Erotic-Sensuous Femininity—
The Exiled Terrain of Sacred Passion, 97*

Dream: A Holy Communion 99
The Harlot: An Ancient Goddess and Her Agents—the Sacred
    Priestess and the Ordinary Prostitute 105
The Sacred Priestess: Votary of the Goddess' Divinity—
    Psychopomp, Mentor, Mediator 114
Can the Feminine Erotic Soul be Redeemed by Modern
    Women? 122

Epilogue: The Reality of the Psyche, 131

A Premonitory Dream 133

Glossary of Jungian Terms 137
Bibliography 143
Index 147
About the Author 153

Foreword

FROM THE OUTSET, Rachel Hillel makes it clear in *The Redemption of the Feminine Erotic Soul* that the quest she is undertaking is motivated as much by her own "soul yearning," as she expresses it, as by the need of her analysands. Despite a secular upbringing on an Israeli kibbutz, she was to experience and to tend in secret (from age 6 or 7) what Jung termed a religious instinct. After a lifetime governed by matters of the heart, she concludes that it was a Love Goddess to whom she prayed for help and guidance, and that she continues to serve to this day.

To this service Rachel Hillel has brought the skills, the discipline, and the understanding of a therapist trained in clinical psychology and in Jungian analysis. Many of the contemporary epiphanies of the Goddess, on which her book is based, come in the form of dream material from her consulting room. In Hillel's view, a large number of these dreams have a collective significance which transcends the situation of the individual dreamer.

The dream images of her women analysands combine sensual passion with religious numinosity. Reflecting the original unity of the ancient feminine cosmogony, the Goddess' sacred vulva and the sacred Priestess, a harlot and healer make their reappearance—not in consciousness, where centuries of monotheism in Western civilization have judged them heretical—but in the unconscious through dreams.

The lack of connection to the instinctual-spiritual roots of these analysands had constellated, in Hillel's view, in a compensatory flow of images from the deepest archetypal layers of the psyche. How these erotic energies may be integrated into consciousness is the challenge posed by this book. Of the importance to each of us and to our time that we meet this challenge, the author leaves little doubt.

—ALICE JOHNSTON
Montreal

Introduction

WE IN OUR Western world are
an Apollonian people living in an Apollonian culture supported
by the structures of the patriarchy. Rational thought—linear,
dialectical, logical—the pattern of Apollonian solar consciousness, has dominated our orientation to ourselves, our relationships with others, and our interaction with our environment.
City skylines mirror our cultural self-definition. We identify with
Wall Street towers of commerce and finance, Ivy League towers
of education, cathedral spires of spiritual life, and government
high-rises of political and judicial policy. These imposing towers,
symbolic of masculine phallic power, remain constantly in our
view—rigid, rectilinear, clean, and cold—and touch every aspect
of our daily life, influencing every conscious thought. No doubt,
they are products of an intellectual struggle that has been important in the evolution of humankind toward mastery. That mastery has, however, been won at great expense to the valuing of
feminine nature.

Feminine lunar consciousness with its diffuse awareness,
instinctual knowledge, wisdom of the heart, its deep roots into
the mysteries of soul and body, the emotional life, and the irrational sources of the creative process, all have been relegated to
an inferior position, as undesirable traits threatening the mastery
of the great world. Those life-enhancing, soul connecting, innate
abilities have been suppressed, repressed, or dismissed as childish.
Yet without the delicate balancing of both masculine and femi-

nine psychologies (in both men and women), we become one-sided or neurotic. The dullness of gender monotony clouds our sensitivity. Mindless time-filling activities replace the play of gender difference, offering momentary reprieve without fulfillment. Substance abuse to ease despair only adds to the confusion and torpor. These banal panaceas of an Apollonian culture cannot replace the healing nature of the feminine, which enhances the well being of the soul.

Counterbalancing the thrusting and penetrating phallus, with its masculine symbolic imagery of stiff, proud, insistence, is the feminine symbolic imagery of the vulva. How very opposite is the vulva's imagery—receiving, enfolding, warm, and moist. How different from the mental or intellectual response, embodied in the psychological principle of the Logos, is the feminine principle of Eros, that of relatedness where chasms of alienation or separateness can be bridged. Instead of competition, we find connectedness; in place of control, there is consensus; rather than coercion, we discover caring.

How does one become reconnected to the instinctive feminine energies? How does one integrate the feminine functions that have been debased and repressed from conscious understanding? How do we as individuals or collectively as a society begin to heal the split-off attributes of Eros? These questions arise as we become more and more conscious of the human condition. Addressing these questions, Dr. Rachel Hillel, Jungian analyst, guides us through personal experiences—her own and those of women analysands—in her account of *The Redemption of the Feminine Erotic Soul.* She opens the door to the realm of the unconscious through dreams, allowing us to view those vital aspects of erotic substance we find incongruous with our collective conscious values. She underscores the importance of the unconscious and how necessary it is for psychic health and wholeness. With skillful perception, she explores the sensuous and erotic aspect of feminine nature—a quality *sine qua non* for women's enlightened self-being. The feminine erotic, not to be thought of as merely sexual, contains the key to this redemption.

C. G. Jung has written, "In each of us there is another whom we do not know. [S]he speaks to us in dreams and tells us how differently [s]he sees us from the way we see ourselves. When, therefore, we find ourselves in a difficult situation to which there is no solution, [s]he can sometimes kindle a light that radically alters our attitude—the very attitude that led us into the difficult situation."[1] Dr. Hillel assists her analysands, and through this book assists her readers, to view the other within each of us whom we do not know. Her work can alter individual and collective attitudes.

I do not believe it is necessary to topple the towers of patriarchy or to repudiate the advances of humankind toward conscious mastery. Yet we need constantly to be aware of the abuse that exists in the repression of feminine nature. That repression is not created by men alone; sadly, women contribute equally to disallowing the true expression of the feminine. Slick magazines, films, anorexic fashion models—all reflect collective ideas that society projects onto women and the image that they must desire to become. How far removed these vague, cool devitalized images are from the full-bodied, radiant, laughter-loving attributes of the goddess of love and beauty! How superficial and lifeless our expressions of sensuousness and eroticism have become.

---

[1] C. G. Jung, *The Collected Works,* vol. 10: *Civilization in Transition,* R. F. C. Hull, trans. (Princeton: Princeton University Press, 1964, 1970), ¶325.

As women become more and more dissociated from instinctive feminine nature they become disempowered.

Can we allow both masculine and feminine attributes to develop, each giving life to the other? The ancient Greeks knew of this necessity in their spiritual life, even when they neglected it in social arrangements. They honored both gods and goddesses, their elaborate temples within sight of one another. Prayers were made to the god of war for courage in battle and to the goddess of love in affairs of the heart. The forces that governed their lives were highly differentiated, but each was honored and sanctified.

We know too well the structures and influence of our culture's orientation toward an Apollonian Logos. The winds are gradually shifting, and in this new climate we are recognizing the necessity of honoring feminine nature. It begins with individuals—-those who are courageous enough to stand against the tyranny of collective thought, those who remain connected to the heart's wisdom, and those who look to the unconscious to redeem that joyous life-giving force—*The Feminine Erotic Soul.*

—NANCY QUALLS-CORBETT

Acknowledgments

I OWE THANKS to my analysands who taught me much and allowed the use of their material.

I am deeply grateful to my three readers: Julia Demmin, Fleur Weymouth, and Clementine Brown. Their ongoing encouragement and insightful commentaries helped me often.

I owe thanks to a special international community—my Jungian colleagues. I am indebted to Marion Woodman, John Beebe, Murray Stein, and Alice Johnston, for assisting me in previous writing projects, and for supporting this one. To Beverly Zabriskie and Joseph Henderson—my gratitude for believing in me. To Andrew Samuels, Robert Bosnak, June Singer, Barbara Koltuv, Jean Shinoda Bolen, Deldon Anne McNeely, and Ann Belford Ulanov for reading the manuscript and endorsing it; to Betty Meador, Daryl Sharp, and Aurora Terrenus for their generous support and kind permission to use their material; to Alice Johnston for writing the foreword; to Nancy Qualls-Corbett my gratitude for writing the introduction.

Over the years I have traveled far and made new friends. I am grateful to the Jung societies that invited me to share my thinking and my writing. I was welcomed everywhere, enjoyed warm hospitality, and learned much from the participants in lectures, seminars, and workshop settings. I am indebted to the following Jung Societies: the Montreal Society for graciously hosting me five times; the Australian Jung Societies in Perth, Adelaide, Melbourne, Sydney, and Canberra, for their generous reception during my two visits; and to the Jung Institutes in Boston, San Francisco, Chicago, and New York, who welcomed me and my work.

My visits to Ottawa, Canada, Thompson, CT, Montpelier, VT, Northhampton, MA, and Washington DC are memorable! I was given the opportunity to present at the Friend's Conference for Religion and Psychology in Haverford, PA, the National Conference of Jungian Analysts in San Francisco, the International Jungian Congress in San Francisco, and at the Israeli Jung Society in Safed.

Material for this book was presented in Mexico City, Mexico, Auckland, New Zealand, and Haifa, Israel. These occasions helped me clarify the text.

I am grateful to my publisher, Betty Lundsted, who patiently provided me with a safe container.

Finally, I am a fortunate woman to be surrounded by a host of guardian angels. I believe most of them are aware of their graceful presence in my life.

Reflections

—◆—

And thou shalt choose life.

—Deuteronomy 30:19

As you start on your journey for Ithaca
then pray that the road is a long one,
full of adventures, full of discovery...

. . . .

May there be many summer mornings when,
with what pleasure, what joy,
you enter harbours you're seeing for the first time;
May you stop at Phoenician trading stations
to buy fine things, mother-of-pearl and coral, amber and ebony,
sensual perfume of every kind—
as many-sensual perfumes as you can;

. . . .

But do not hurry the voyage at all.
Better if it lasts for years...
...by the time you reach the island
wealthy with all you have gained on the way

With the great wisdom you have gained, with so much experience
you must surely have understood by then what Ithaca means

—"Ithaca," C. P. Cavafy

I enter a dark church, lit with candles,
I hear a voice, "God does not understand Jung."
I then look up and see my analyst, sitting on a bal-
  cony, which reminds me of the Romeo and Juliet
  balcony scene.
She says to me: "The true Divine is Eros."

—PAMELA'S DREAM (A FORMER NUN)

Jung appears and tells me: Look and see
There are two roads in life
One is the Natural road
It has a tree.
The other is the Spiritual road
It has a cross
At the ends both roads meet.

—KATHERINE'S DREAM (A SCIENTIST)

The Inborn Religious Instinct—
Confessing an Early Experience
of the Goddess

Called or not called, the Goddess shall be there.

—THE DELPHIC TEMPLE ORACLES

Now Faith is the promise of things hoped for, the evidence of things not seen.

—(HEBREWS 11:1)[1]

I WAS BORN and raised on an Israeli kibbutz, an enlightened secular commune, a structure which was guided by moral and social ideals. When I was a little girl, I was repeatedly told by the people who raised me that there is no God. I never doubted these honorable people, so I believed this important statement as well. These were, after all, my loyal guardians, men and women devoted to visionary idealism.

Surrounded by an unqualified trust in the perfectibility of human life through scientific, economic, and social progress, I was reassured, time and again, that all phenomena are to be comprehended strictly within a rational-logical frame of reference. Obviously, within the commune's ideological structure, unknown psychic realities either did not exist, were considered irrational, or were at best shrugged off as obsolete.

---

[1]This and all other biblical references in this book are from the Authorized King James Version (Oxford: Oxford University Press, n.d.) for I felt that most readers would be familiar with this translation.

The kibbutz provided no room for reverence and awe toward the mysterious. Transcendent realms were not present; holiness was inaccessible; the sense of numinosity was alien. Thus the domain of the sublime, an entire area of human knowledge, remained repressed. Of course, no indoctrination can intrude upon a child's sense of amazement and rich imagination, but it can certainly interfere with it and split off living experiences from consciousness.

Therefore it was unexpected that a sense of the sacred would emerge spontaneously in me, independent of external influences. During my tender childhood, at 6 or 7, I was awakened into a terrain of soul yearning and knew this part of myself required frequent tending. I knew instinctively that my discoveries required a ritual, even though I had not yet been exposed to the various religious rituals that exist in history. They were, *de facto*, my personal declarations of faith. At that time, I was unfamiliar with archetypal concepts such as "Divinity," or "Holiness." Still, in praxis, I embraced these concepts and lived them out.

Moreover, I instinctively understood that my unutterable longings must be sheltered, never spoken of to anyone. By carefully selecting a secluded site for my private ritual, I intuitively shaped a vessel where I could nurture my soul. No one had any idea of my activities, as I carefully chose a remote place, a spacious meadow hidden behind an apple orchard. This safe, earthly temple consisted of opposing backgrounds, the openly-lit field enclosed by dark trees.

I knelt and prayed often. Again and again I pleaded for assistance and guidance. I tested the validity of my hopes by plucking flower petals, anticipating that my innocent attitude, suffused with devotion, would enhance a desired outcome, a realization of my soul yearnings which were projected on my early loves, my tender infatuations. My supplication was directed at a female figure, a Gracious Lady. Compelled by strange urges, I made a commitment to serve Her in activities for which I had no name.

Who evoked the conviction, the persistence, the faith? Who invoked and initiated me? Who designed a holy private shrine which I shared with no one? I did not comprehend the nature of the compulsion, but I obediently surrendered, protecting its fragility through secrecy. I realized it must not be violated or belittled. I know now that the zealous hiding of my secret was based on appropriate instinctual fears lest my psyche be desecrated, my religious longings trampled upon.

Today, decades later, my worship site has vanished. As the commune expanded, both field and orchards were replaced with buildings. That field and orchard belong only to the private intangible domain of my innermost early memories. The place of my early worship retains a unique and numinous quality in my heart.

I often reflect on the psychological significance of my religious life at such a young age. I respect the stubborn fierce sense of containing the entire experience in great silence. My personal experience, springing in defiance of secular upbringing, validates an important tenet of Jung's. We are born with a desire to find meaning in life, which Jung called a religious instinct. This religious instinct is an archetypal psychic pattern that emerges autonomously, comparable to the biological instinct, an innate tendency to imbue existence with significance. In the absence of traditional rituals of worship, and the loss of environmental models, personal containers can nevertheless be established. Directed by psychic inner commands, spontaneous constellations of religiosity emerge when outer gods are banished. My childhood fascination surprises me no more. As an adult, I believe in the existence of an innate urge to connect intimately with a deity, a transpersonal center of the Self.

As a little girl, this drive manifested itself in an image of a Goddess. Who was this deity whom I contacted in the midst of an atheist-pastoral setting? For whom was the temple of my tender passions erected? Matters of the heart, the Eros realm, have forever been central themes in my life. Most certainly it was a Love Goddess to whom I prayed; a supreme deity in charge of Love made me kneel and entreat Her for support and guidance.

Long ago, so early, independent of will or choice, I was destined to commence a soul journey in quest of Her, the Goddess.

> *She wears*
> *the carved-out grand plan*
> *of heaven and earth.*
>
> *She goes out*
> *white-sparked, radiant*
> *in the dark vault of the evening sky*
> *star-steps in the street*
> *through the Gate of Wonder.*[2]

---

[2]"Inanna and Ebeh," poem to the Goddess Inanna, incribed by her High Priestess Enheduanna, circa 4300 years ago. This rendition by Betty Meador, in a lecture, "First Poet in the World," San Francisco, 1988. Used by kind permission.

CHAPTER ONE

*An Awakening into the
Modern Feminine Quandary*

Dream: Jung and the Vulva

This song is holy.
Let me tell you where
*   I am coming from.*
My vulva is
the power place
a royal sign.

I rule with vulva power
I see with vulva eyes
This is where
I am coming from.

Fit me out
with my vulva
I live right there
In this soft slit
I live right there.

My field wants hoeing
This is my holy word.

Vulva Song

I, the lady
in this house of holy lapis
in sanctuary I pray
I say a holy prayer

I am the Queen of Heaven

let my bridegroom rejoice with me

I Inanna sing to praise him
I give him my vulva song

peg my vulva
my star/sketched horn of the Dipper
moor my slender boat of heaven
my new moon crescent vulva beauty

I wait an unplowed desert
fallow field for the wild ducks
my high mound longs for the footlands

my vulva hill is open
this maid asks who will plow it

vulva moist in the footlands
the king, Lady, will plow it

plow then man of my heart
hold water-bathed loins.[1]

SUSAN, a Jungian candidate in the final stages of her formal training, entered her analytical hour, narrating the following dream.

Jung is old and frail. His whole manner reflects fatigue and the renunciation of worldly matters. There he is, lying on a bare floor in a spare room, all skin and bones. It is obvious that he is dying.

I stand beside him, determined to cooperate and assist in every possible way in prolonging his life. Suddenly Jung asks to put the palm of his hand in my vagina. Without words he is pleading with me, communicating despairingly that the vagina's warmth is his last resort, indeed his lifeline to keep him alive and revive him.

This non-verbal imploring I clearly understand. Even though completely taken aback, even shocked, I cooperate with his request, overcoming great reservations.

After a short time of holding his hand in my vagina, it becomes apparent that Jung is not merely kept alive, but rather greatly improved. Shortly thereafter, he is completely healed.

---

[1] Two poems, written about 2500 B.C. in Mesopotamia. "The Sacred Marriage Ritual," rendition by Betty Meador in *Uncursing the Dark* (Wilmette: Chiron, 1992), pp. 59–60. Used by kind permission.

Susan was disgusted and repulsed: "I find the dream's setting and themes incredible. An elderly, cultivated gentleman, most celebrated and revered! How can Jung express such uncontrollable lust. Such uncouth behavior for a man of his stature!"

Susan's emotional commentary ended her engagement with the dream. She was probing for personal associations but could not provide any. "No," sighed Susan, "there is really no point to further discuss or explore this strange dream." I accepted her wish. It was her analytical hour, to be respected.

Thus, the untended-to dream remained untouched. I had listened carefully and had known right away that this was no ordinary dream. It heralded a powerful pronouncement.

The initial question, unanswerable but deserving serious consideration, surrounded the dream's boundaries. The dream calls for an urgent, unmitigated intervention. Whenever a dream declares an emergency, depicting a state of *extremis*, it is crucial to decipher its aim, its transpersonal significance. "What areas are pronounced in terminal ill-health?" Obviously, an "old king" appears gravely ill, symbolizing an anachronistic value system. A psychic imbalance was indicated. By whom? Does the dream content refer exclusively to Jungian analytical psychology, conveying a state of waning vigor, perhaps profound doubts concerning its basic tenets? Perhaps the dream mirrors a greater state of malaise? There is no doubt that the dream depicts an all-pervasive crisis, possibly a collapse of masculine principles concerning the spirit. The monotheistic values constitute the "dis-ease," an imbalanced arid Logos framework, lacking Eros' moisture. The dream conveys a statement that masculine spiritual Western contents are in grave danger of annihilation, as personified by Jung's critical condition.

Above all, what is the psychological meaning of the curative symbol, as indicated by the dream? Not only does the dream insist on the urgency of the treatment, it also articulates a distinctive qualitative prescription. The exhausted masculine values must be rescued.

Paradoxically, an alchemical tenet directs the solution: the remedy is to be discovered within an antithetical realm, in the opposite feminine container. After millennia of animosity and deep distrust a resuscitation is to be sought within the quintessential feminine vessel. The feminine supplies the precisely required measures capable of preventing masculine spiritual extinction. Trust must be regained if change is to take place. A leap of faith must alter the age-old alienation between the contrary realms—the feminine and the masculine.

Why is the vagina chosen by the dream?

The purpose is to alarm—even to shock—the dreamer into awakening. Had the dream elected a lesser female organ, less risqué, less dramatic, its message would become diluted and elude awareness. Furthermore, the vagina symbol conveys a distinct intentionality. Indeed the vagina is, psychologically, of momentous significance.

The vagina is a present-day term for the vulva, a principal symbol within the mythological repository of ancient Goddesses. The Goddesses, identified with Nature, encompassed Nature's entire range of powers. Nature endowed the various Goddesses with inherent sovereignty above all existence. The Goddess' dignity was located in her vulva, as documented in the earliest written records. The vulva was, above all else, a sacred place imbued with divine meaning. The Goddess' vulva connoted a primordial place of female power—the seat of life's affirmation, an abode of desirousness and ecstatic passions.

The most intimate contact with the feminine matrix is commanded by the unconscious. According to the dream, the archetypal masculine values of the spirit must urgently connect to the vulva, the core of ancient feminine consciousness, in order for healing to take place. The active reaching out by the masculine into the female essence, the vulva, is of vital importance. Without the crucial feminine to balance the collective patriarchal principle, psychic reality becomes barren. The vulva alone, or rather what it symbolizes, can cure the ailing king.

Jung, a king, corresponds to the masculine barren ego that must be ill or wounded in order to open up to feminine unconscious contents. The "wounds" have a positive meaning. Eventually this very illness, or "woundedness," promotes psychic renewal. Within feminine interiority, the masculine is to be renewed. Most alien to the masculine, the vulva has been the focus of terror for the masculine domain. Its "otherness" has been a target for negative projections and has betrayed fears of its sacred numinosity, its place as a seat of *mana*. A coeval place of moist darkness and life's conception, the vulva has been dreaded and, consequently, ignored by the Western psyche. Spirit has deluded itself that it can deny, crush, and transcend Nature.

Prompted by the Self, this dream insists on a renewed kinship to life's *élan vital* through feminine earth-sensuality. The dream yields a collective message whose significance transcends the individual dreamer. The dream's teleos, its purposeful meaning, is a statement. It is a containment within transpersonal feminine powers that can restore sacredness to an impoverished spirit which had shriveled into an intellect. Erotic-sensuality, divine passion, the mystery and vigor of the vulva carry the hope of transformative restoration for the "ailing King."

Dream: Healing the Wounded Vulva

•═━►◆◄━═•

Without consideration, without pity, without shame
  they have built big and high walls around me

. . .

And now I sit here despairing.
  I think of nothing else: the fate gnaws at my mind;

. . .

Ah, why didn't I observe them when they were
  building the walls?

. . .

But I never heard the noise or the sound of the
  builders.
Imperceptibly they shut me out of the world.[2]

NORA, a professional woman, is an accomplished and successful psychotherapist. She has an excellent reputation as a conscientious practitioner who is earnest and devoted to her work. Her tailored self-image exudes equanimity and trustworthiness, qualities admired and counted upon by many. No one has an idea of the mounting pressure exerted in order to create Nora's calm composure. The tight exercise of self-control, the masked oppression, the emotional denials, all pass undetected, well-protected.

---

[2]C. P. Cavafy, "Walls" in *The Complete Poems of Cavafy,* Rae Dalven, ed. Copyright © 1961, renewed 1987 by Rae Dalven. Reprinted by permission of Harcourt Brace & Company, Orlando, and Hogarth Press, London.

Left with little time or energy for herself, Nora's vocation has gradually become all consuming, surrounding her by "big and high walls" that have separated her from life's spontaneous flow. Children, family, friends, all must wait, aware that they come second, are less crucial to Nora's sense of well-being.

Nora cannot just allow life to happen. Rather, she speaks with zealot-theoretical certainty about life. Nora's predicament is impersonal. Unknowingly, she is an engaged member, an active participant in the collective one-sidedness of modern-day feminists. Intoxicated by a sense of mission, contemporary deliverers, Nora and her colleagues tend to see themselves as crusaders in noble causes. Possessed people have no awareness of their state of bondage, the psychological state of emotional subjugation.

Unfettered by external oppression and no longer shackled by social constrictions, women now are in danger of enslaving themselves to conscious ideology. Their guiding values are "independence," "self-fulfillment," "self-realization"; their vitality is harnessed to their careers. Victims rather than rulers of their destinies, unsupported by an instinctual-earthy sense of groundedness in their feminine nature, Nora and her colleagues are psychologically uprooted. In the grip of an unconscious complex, a possession by their inner masculine side, they are devoured at present by obsessive ambitions.

Severed from the feminine sensual matrix, these women not only betray Eros, but, most of all, they abandon the sacred vulva, the archetypal seat of ecstatic delights and life's joyful affirmation. Sadly, the feminine has been sacrificed again, this time by liberated feminists, driven by a sense of "duty" and "no play."

On Nora's 50th birthday the usual seven-hour workload was maintained and generous attention was paid to each client. At the end of her workday, exhausted by a wholehearted renouncing of herself, there was nothing left. Discouraged, lonely, and empty, Nora's shadow side of her magnanimity took over. It was provoked to action by the desperate need to maintain a sense of control by keeping others gratefully dependent.

It had not occurred to Nora to spend her birthday lavishly, splurging and pleasing herself. Nora had never considered the psychological meaning of a birthday celebration as a self-respecting joyful reminder, a ritual honoring one's inherent loveliness. Everyone deserves to be special. Celebrating a birthday is one's birthright, not a vain self-indulgence. Turning 50 marks an end to a decade, and, more importantly, it circumscribes the final phase of being middle-aged.

After many years of ignoring her special annual day, Nora's psyche finally rebelled against the neglect, the defiance and violation of Nature's psychological laws. The scene that ensued compensated for Nora's lack of conscious participation. Instead, her unconscious conveyed its protest in an autonomous fashion. It arranged a shadowy way to give voice to this special 50th birthday.

The eruption, so unexpected, seemingly entirely unjustified, so remote from Nora's habitual demeanor, lasted a long time. Nora's various "walls" totally collapsed as she lay on the floor; sobbing, wailing, yelling, shrieking, screaming.

Bewildered, she wished only to rid herself of the humiliating memories. Impatient with the entire event, eager to forget it, Nora asked no questions concerning the rage and venom that engulfed her. The event was so embarrassing that she did not wish to explore its psychological meaning. When she arrived a few days later for our analytic session, Nora expressed sincere regrets for this "awful, absurd, ridiculous relapse. I was seized by an explosive temper tantrum, being at the mercy of an hysterical fit, that is all. It does not make any sense," she commented.

Nora did not understand the abrupt upheaval nor did she feel compassion toward this desperate, lowly, "creaturely" behavior. What had taken place was not perceived as an aspect of herself. Rejecting the unbidden event, she was too scared to look inward and observe the storm arranged by a split part of herself, an unsolicited response to self-denial and starvation.

Toward the end of our session Nora mentioned casually that after her "fit," that same night, she had a dream. She proceeded to narrate it.

> Unannounced, my healer, Mary, paid a professional call to my house, even though I did not summon her. Nor does she ever pay home visits. Mary attended to my condition, applying a syringe to my vagina. She injected a gentle substance four times at evenly spaced points, thus forming the shape of a cross. Her touch felt cozy and wonderfully soothing. As I woke up, I felt a sense of comfort and great peace.

Mary, a healer whom Nora visited regularly, saw clients in her home, which was located in a remote hilltown. Nora described Mary as being endowed with remarkable healing talents. It was obvious that Nora found Mary's involvement with her vocation similar to the way Nora felt about hers. Nora focused on the priorities that guided Mary's daily routine: "A spiritual mode of living imbued Mary's physical environs with tranquillity. Mary believes that a state of grace is the source of her healing power, and, she, in turn, is called upon to act as an accountable guardian of her gifts. The necessity to nurture and take care of herself in order to balance the demands made on her by others is foremost on her list.

"Mary's life is determined by making choices geared at maintaining psychic balance; these choices she guards as rules with no exceptions. Strict about retiring early to her bed, Mary rises before dawn to devote quiet hours to prayer and meditation. Noon hours become rest periods, during which Mary walks, gardens, writes, dances, sings, and plays music.

"It is pleasant to approach Mary's house. Serenity permeates the surrounding fields. There is a stillness that is so pure about her exquisite flower and vegetable gardens. Her sessions are experienced by some as the transmutation of an hour into a sacred ritual."

Nora's associations to Mary greatly assisted in deciphering the psychological meaning behind the dream. Unlike Nora, Mary offered and received spiritual sustenance. Through personal integrity Mary established, and maintained, a wholesome mode of living in tune with her inner needs.

Nora was given a magnificent, perfect gift on her 50th birthday! The dream provided a resolution to her profound distress by way of mending her inner split. Nora's psyche compensated for her alienated attitude by clearly indicating that she must cure her neglected femininity. In a present-day efficient ego like Nora's, a feminine earthy center—a vessel of sanctified sensuality—is absent. The sacred vulva, the place where sensuality and sacredness are reconciled, needs to be healed. Mary enacted the archetypal role of a sacred priestess and applied a balm to Nora's wounded vulva through the injections.

The cross, a symbol where opposites unite, represents the spiritual potential for psychic wholeness. Nora's dream heralds a vital statement about the contemporary deprivation suffered by modern women because of their rejection of erotic-sensual femininity.

A new beginning was announced for Nora on her 50th birthday. Her dream proclaimed a rebirth and offered a transformative experience. Initiated into a wholesome way of being by Mary's healing, Nora's vulva, a sacred feminine place, was awakened, calling her to partake of life's wholesome affirmation.

Big Dreams: For Whom Are They Dreamed?

A natural bridge is erected between the Hebrew word חֲלוֹם = *khalom* = dream and הַחְלָמָה = *hakhlama* = healing via the commonality of their triliteral roots. The etymological ties are meaningful. They connote a guidance, a healing opportunity through dreamwork. The personal choice of whether or not to cross the bridge erected by nature in Hebrew etymology remains the task of each individual.

In a dream, in a vision of the night, when deep sleep falleth upon men, in slumberings upon the bed; Then He openeth the ears of men, and sealeth their instruction.

—(JOB 33:15–16)

. . . a dream is a theatre in which the dreamer is himself the scene, the player, the prompter, the producer, the author, the public, and the critic.[3]

JUNGIAN psychotherapy, my vocation, concerns itself with the subjective expression of an

---

[3]C. G. Jung, *Collected Works*, vol. 8, ¶509.

individual psyche. Dreams are an innate expression of the dreamer's psyche. Do all dreams pertain exclusively to the dreamer? Are all dreams brought to therapy by an individual dreamer intended solely to be strictly personal messages?

Every analyst has thought about this topic time and again. Of course, there are no absolute answers. An enigmatic quality is part of all phenomena pertaining to the human psyche. Still, since dreams are "daily bread" for analysts, we all make observations. I have come to believe in the existence of significant dreams, "big dreams," for they open a door to universal spiritual experiences.

These "big dreams" transmit transpersonal archetypal contents and bear valuable information. An autonomous source conveys vital messages to the collective psyche. When one of the "big dreams" occurs, the dreamer usually has few associations and refrains from interpretations, claiming that the material is alien to her reality and elicits no personal connections. The analyst must respect the analysand's right not to discuss her dream. Thus the dream material remains untouched. "Big dreams" usually retain their virginal character, untended by conscious intervention. Of course, not all undiscussed dreams are "big dreams."

I have often observed that the "big dream" symbols may serve as an acknowledgment of an objective situation that exists in the collective psyche, and thus may reinforce an already familiar state. These dreams may point to new directions or future tendencies through an unraveling and deciphering of general societal predicaments. Some "big dreams" may provide alternative guidelines to the prevailing impasses in the community.

Such dreams may also offer other paths than the already prevailing methods through an *enantiodromia*. Thus, "big dreams" can convey compensatory themes to those existing already in collective consciousness. These dreams emerge from the unconscious in opposition to current conscious attitudes and may provide creative solutions to contemporaneous bewilderment. Such "big dreams" possess a transpersonal authority to alleviate a communal malaise. They offer instruction regarding necessary changes in the conscious attitude of the collective. Big transformative dreams are harbingers of redemption. I have come to believe that a "big dream," with all its characteristic qualities, might prove a messenger, a courier of prominent and premonitory intelligence. If the "big dreams" are not discussed, the analyst has to determine whether or not to interpret the coded messages to the dreamer.

Further, I have come to believe, and dare to state, that sometimes these "big dreams" are dreamed, in part, for the analyst's sake, carrying meaningful insights and perceptions for her benefit. These dreams touch on pertinent dilemmas in the analyst's psyche about which the dreamer-analysand has no conscious knowledge. The analyst then experiences such dreams as a synchronistic event.

Are we analysts assisted in our developmental processes by our analysands? Surely clinical terms such as "transference-countertransference" are limited, too scant to convey adequately the intricate exchanges between analyst and analysand, the subtle metamorphoses which transpire respectively during the course of the unique analytical relationship. Our analysand's dreams may become our rewards, for they bring additional challenges for our own inner tasks.

In general, dreams brought into sessions deserve to be listened to earnestly and attentively by the analyst. Careful discernment ought to be paid as well vis-à-vis the personal meaning for the analyst. The personal meaning for the analyst is not to be discussed with the analysand. Rather it is understood in quiet analytical privacy. If there is a lack of consciousness by the analyst and dreams are ignored, the unconscious impact may result in destructive impact on the analyst's psyche. Unconsciousness, as we all know, is a less fortunate choice.

de Profundis: The Purpose of the Work

—◄❖►—

The term "Religion" designates the attitude peculiar to
a consciousness which has been changed by experience
of the numinosum.[4]

> *Share with me*
> *this myth told so long ago*
> *that I only heard today*
> *of the possibilities of a beginning,*
> *of an ending begun long long ago.*[5]

"NUMINOSITY" refers to experi-
ences of a sacred dimension which points to an ultimate reality.
It is archetypal; its shared meaning reappears universally in the
human collective, and yet it is unique to each person. The experience of the sacred, the numinous, is therefore an innate ele-
ment in the structure of human consciousness.

The Jewish Passover Haggadah, the time-honored retelling
of the numinous events in Exodus (Yetziass Mitzraim), is con-
ducted in the spirit of instruction. Furthermore, a command is
given to all guests who gather to celebrate the annual Seder feast:

---

[4]C. G. Jung, *Collected Works,* vol. 11, ¶9.
[5]Aurora Terrenus, *The Shroud of Sophia* (Santa Cruz, CA: Celestial, 1988), p. 6. Used by
kind permission.

"In every generation every person must feel as if he himself came out of Egypt."

Adding to this statement the frequency in which the "Redemption from Egypt" theme is mentioned in the course of daily orthodox routine (e.g., the Sabbath benediction, or *Kiddush*, the daily laying of *Tefilin,* or phylacteries, on the head and hands, the morning and evening prayer services, to mention just a few customs within Jewish tradition), makes it clear that the "Redemption from Egypt" represents a major archetypal symbol, a universal motif that transcends the exclusivity of the patriarchal faith. Its meaning reflects an eternal theme with whose significance one must identify, a theme that is alive in each individual psyche.

"In every generation," connotes a continual remembrance of the event called the "Redemption from Egypt," for the event is as significant now as it was to our ancestors. It must be experienced as if we ourselves have lived to see it. The Exodus archetype is a psychic reality for everyone. Its theme is concerned with an active liberation from a state of "slavery." Psychologically, "slavery" connotes unconsciousness. The Exodus myth symbolizes the heroic struggle involved in the process of becoming conscious, including the temptation to return to unconsciousness. The regressive "go back to Egypt" tendencies that are expressed in the myth of Exodus refer to everyone's childlike desire for a dependency that requires no responsibility or accountability. For these psychological reasons, the "Redemption from Egypt" remains an indispensable symbol, pertinent and alive in every psyche.

The Haggadah's insistence "in every generation" serves as an apt metaphor, in both scope and magnitude, for the ongoing transformation now taking place within feminine consciousness.

For it is "in our generation," that psychic contents of numinous dimensions emerge from the collective unconscious to collective consciousness in the Western world for modern women. It is not merely a collective challenge. Consciousness concerning the emerging unconscious numinous contents is a simultaneous personal requisite as well.

Reclaiming an individual relationship to numinous images of the "archetypal feminine," connecting to the heritage of the Goddess' cosmogony, is a collective and personal task that requires examining the eternal living symbols constellated within each psyche "in our generation." The mending of severed contents and the conscious integration of archetypal themes amounts to the "redemption of the feminine" from its involuntary bondage in an unconscious state.

Buried in the unconscious of the monotheistic framework for two millennia, feminine numinous energies burst forth and rise to the surface, emerging from exile into communal and individual awareness. The autonomous reawakening of transpersonal feminine contents at present is therefore a collective opus as well as an individual opus. It furthers the unearthing of hitherto split-off psychic layers. We rediscover within our individual psyche the inner aliveness of feminine symbols, such as the Goddess' sacred vulva. Her erotic-sensual soul passions signify an initiation into Her sacred mysteries.

This book was written to clarify erotic-sensual psychic themes that constitute only a particular aspect within the entire archetypal feminine matrix. Hallowed within ancient feminine cosmology, erotic-sensual energies have not yet been differentiated and explored sufficiently.

The earliest documented records, dating from Paleolithic and Neolithic aeons, center around Mesopotamia, Babylon,

Sumeria, the Near East and parts of southern Europe. They consist, in the main, of archeological excavations which chronicle a Goddess as supreme deity. Ancient cultures, ruled by feminine archetypes, lasted about 25,000 years as compared with 3,000–4,000 years of later masculine sovereignty.[6]

Among the various archetypal representations of female deities that existed in the remote past, the archetypal image of the Love Goddess embodied a dynamic transformative principle. The Love Goddess' rituals transferred its participants' souls into sublime realms by means of erotic-sensual passion. The Goddess' worshippers venerated erotic-sensual sacredness. Its constellation was perceived as a numinous divine blessing. Priestesses served as holy mentors in the Goddess' temples where Her mysteries were revealed to devoted initiates. The priestess' teaching glorified erotic-sensual vitality. The human body was viewed as a shrine for the passionate desires of the soul, a holy container. Regeneration through sexual acts was sanctified.[7]

Of all feminine elements, erotic-sensuality, innately supported by Nature and earthly instinctuality, by definition has been most polarized to masculine consciousness. It represented an extreme opposite to an ideology that adored the spirit, an abstract male God. The inherent dichotomy between the original feminine cosmogony, and the later masculine cosmogony posed an existential threat to the survival of the newly established and still fragile monotheistic faith.

The monotheistic paradigm introduced new principles that served the objective evolution of human consciousness. Initially aimed at securing its brittle identity, it produced a negation by

---

[6]Betty Meador, *Uncursing the Dark* (Wilmette, IL: Chiron, 1992), p. 136.
[7]Anne Baring and Jules Cashford, *The Myth of the Goddess* (London: Penguin, 1991), pp. 197–199.

creating its extreme opposite, projecting all "evil" on the Goddess, while maintaining a one-sided "goodness." The masculine thrust to elaborate ideas concerning expansion of the laws of the spirit logos, ego functioning, and ethics became the prerequisite for the progress of civilization. The masculine worldview introduced new paradigms which served the objective evolution of human consciousness.

At that phase of the masculine worldview, it was necessary to defeat or overcome the feminine goddess. The Goddess' numinosity was withdrawn, enveloped in the collective unconscious. This mode of two opposite poles lasted through millennia of archetypal masculine consciousness, while the Goddess remained in the unconscious, a concurrent archetypal feminine.

Erotic-sensual potency, which precedes and surpasses the spiritual tendencies within humankind, was vehemently persecuted by the patriarchy. Fear produced compensatory desecrations, culminating in the abolition of feminine power in general, and erotic-sensuality in particular. Cast into the dark recesses of Western unconsciousness by the monotheistic faith, the archetypal essence of feminine erotic-sensual psychic contents remained ignored and repressed for many centuries.

These archetypal layers constitute erotic-sensual themes, and they belong in the transpersonal part of the psyche. They are shared by all humans. A restoration of split-off transpersonal contents to consciousness is defined as a religious undertaking when the purpose of religion is understood as an integration (Latin *religere* = binding, tying) of transpersonal contents; hence its perception as a task termed "redemption." Acceptance of erotic-sensual femininity as an integral part of psychic wholeness—the Self—is a religious redemptive goal. It involves a transformation in modern-day consciousness.

A Jewish Kabbalistic paradigm narrates a mystical vision concerning a primordial catastrophe. A grand shattering caused a tragic fall of the holy sparks from their inherent state of illuminated grace unto the ground. The sacred vessels, serving as containers for the emanating rays of light, were no longer able to contain the brilliance of the lights. They broke down and shattered. Consequently their contents, the holy sparks, scattered through the cosmos, and became trapped in material existence. The Kabbalistic teaching challenges its devotees to partake in a religious mission, a human task of redemption. "Restoring" the scattered sparks from their entanglement in matter into their former pristine state of divinity, is accomplished through *tiqqun* ("mending, repairing"). The Kabbalistic tiqqun is psychologically meaningful. It implies the mending of an inner split, the repair of an inner severance, when unconscious contents are integrated through conscious efforts.

By analogy, the process of conscious integration of feminine erotic-sensual components, sanctified ancient archetypes, can be likened to the Kabbalistic "raising of the fallen holy sparks." Repressed, split-off, they, too, are trapped in the collective unconscious matter. Their elevation unto their former dignity through memory of the psychic split is a tiqqun. In spite of the autonomous emergence of erotic-sensual contents, their sacred value has not as yet received an appropriate acknowledgment by the women's movement.

History can be assessed from an evolutionary perspective that axiomatically assumes inner-directed, self-determined developmental tendencies toward greater consciousness. This point of view measures the masculine monotheism through criteria of eliciting ego awareness, human ethics, the development of logos framework, and its emphasis on spiritual values. In order to accomplish these advancements, the oppression of the feminine can seem warranted and necessary. The inevitable hostility that transpired toward the feminine can be understood as a compensatory historical inevitability. Dualistic conceptions which divide units into radical opposites tend to run their historical course. The evolution of consciousness elicits either a compensation, a resurgence of the repressed material, or allows for a dialogue between the opposites, while they are both held in consciousness.

It can be stated, however, that by observing the emergence to consciousness of feminine values, new developmental tendencies also can manifest themselves autonomously, in accordance with the historical evolutionary perspective. The reawakening of feminine images, in general, exacts a renewed consciousness of the ancient venerated themes surrounding the Goddess' passions. (The restoration of the ancient dignity of the sacred vulva and of its passionate erotic-sensual feminine energies is a current task.) Heirs to the monotheistic legacy, the exclusivity of either a feminine or a masculine frame of reference is no longer appropriate for the Western contemporary psyche. Today's reality calls for psychic wholeness—a totality. Thus, a synthesis, a union of opposites—the feminine and masculine—is required. Bearing opposites in consciousness creates a constructive tension, a prerequisite for genuine relatedness. An apt symbolic representation of our highest values, a modern archetype of the Supreme Deity, is mandatory. It must reinclude feminine archetypes, encompassing erotic-sensual images as well. The sanctification of the desecrated archetypal psychic contents as an integral part of contemporary deity amounts to redemption, consistent with the Kabbalistic paradigm where "fallen" material is restored and raised to its original holiness.

CHAPTER TWO

*Homeward: An Inauguration into
Feminine Sensuality—The
Goddess' Veiled Reality*

Epiphany: The Showing Forth

———◆———

Therefore I prayed
and understanding was given me.[1]

You, the lady...
When you cast your eyes upon the land,
there is rain and overflow.
When you have cast your eye upon the man
life is long for him.[2]

ONE CAN become aware, but never fully conscious, of feminine sensuality, since the Goddess' nature is forever veiled. Always an enigma, unfathomable, the Goddess' secrets are sealed. Behind the veil lifted, boundless other veils remain.

Once, during Epiphany week, I stumbled upon the wealth of feminine sensuality. Four of the Goddess' veils were lifted during the week. Unannounced, I encountered four occasions, four separate events, seemingly unrelated, which together, formed a coherent quaternity.

Epiphany is a religious church celebration which commemorates the manifestation of Christ in the persons of the Magi. In

---

[1] "Wisdom of Solomon" 7:7 in *The Apocrypha of the Old Testament,* Revised Standard Version (London & New York: Thomas Nelson and Sons, 1957).
[2] The Gudea Cylinder carries this Sumerian hymn, inscribed about 2100 B.C. (The Louvre, Paris). From S. N. Kramer's *The Sacred Marriage Rite* (Bloomington, IN: Indiana University Press, 1969), p. 54.

Greek and Latin, *epiphania* connotes "an appearance," "an apparition," "the showing forth."

Epiphany week is suffused with extraordinary manifestations: holy spectacles, divine incarnations, miraculous events, all illuminate the season's bleakness. The advent of light bringers, Lucifers of all kinds, make up an annual elating gift for disheartened souls, whose gloom stems from the harsh reality of midwinter darkness. The uplifting visitations of deities are eagerly anticipated at this time of year.

A few years ago it was not God that epiphany's "showing forth" elected to manifest for me. Rather, a Goddess was manifested, a female deity in all her glorious sensual features, a surprising visitation, not at all anticipated. I was to discover that each of the four adventures offered a partial unveiling of the Goddess' erotic-sensual realm. It entreated me to go on and keep searching Her enigmatic secrets. A feminine arena, tightly sealed, summoned a further quest.

> *I come forth like a queen*
>
> . . .
>
> *Praise my way.*
> *Praise me!*
>
> . . .
>
> *Listen to my words...*
> *proclaimed through heart...*
> *I come forth a queen...*
>
> . . .
>
> *Lady of the largest heart*
> *in all lands supreme.*[3]

---

[3]Temple hymn to the Sumerian Goddess Inanna, written by her High Priestess Enheduanna, 4300 years ago. Rendition by Betty Meador in a lecture, "First Poet in the World," given in 1988 in San Francisco. Used by kind permission.

The Gazebo: Vistas from an Enchanted Pavilion

—◦—

Her clothing is silk and purple.

—(PROVERBS 31:22)

ON A lovely crisp New England morning I drove to town, a long list of errands in my purse, heading initially to a local bookbinder. My conscious plan then was to enhance knowledge, symbolized by the preservation of precious books. Books have always been a source of inspiration for me.

On the way, things changed, electing an autonomous course. My unconscious designed to halt my narrow ego pursuits, my one-sided focusing on intellectual and conceptual interests. "Amen," resonated my psyche, "It is high time for other vistas to open."

As I drove, I passed a fancy lingerie store I had never noticed before although I had passed it routinely. Deep-seated prejudices must have been blinding, those memories that taught women that "beauty is vain"(Proverbs 31:30) apparently prevented my seeing the prominent sign, "Gazebo," until now.

I never made it to the bookbinder. In fact, the entire list of errands faded away. I entered the Gazebo. Spellbound, I was instantly transported to an earthly paradise. A great variety of refined textures and colors bewitched me, a feast to the tactile and visual senses. The radiant beauty and the luxury everywhere were stunning, luring me into touching and trying on an abundance of the finest linen, silk and lace for hours. A daring color profusion, an entire array of shades and hues, unfolded before my eyes: the regal glow of gold and silver, voluptuous iridescent brilliance, pale, soothing tones. The broad spectrum of colors created an intoxicating momentum. Bewitched, enthralled by the discovery of the Gazebo, a name that connotes great vistas, I alternated between looking, touching, trying on garments, and buying.

I recovered an exiled feminine region. My soul echoed with profound joy as I opened myself to reclaim a lost terrain, celebrating an alliance with the Goddess. I was a woman transformed, reborn. My birthright, which inherently belonged to me, the freedom to delight in an entrancing realm, shut off for so long, was finally granted me.

My psyche consented to this late initiation, permitting me to surrender to numinous powers. Each of us, when ready, finds her private key to unlock the gateway to the Goddess' shrine.

Another Goddess Worshipper

Ointment and perfume rejoice the heart.

—(PROVERBS 27:9)

How fair is thy love, my sister, my spouse! How much better is thy love than wine! And the smell of thine ointments than spices!

—(SOLOMON'S SONG 4:10)

THE SECOND significant event during Epiphany week was a visit to a New York skincare salon. There is nothing exceptional about an appointment with a recommended beautician. Yet, unexpectedly I encountered a devoted priestess of the Goddess. Miriam, of Greek origin, was by no means an ordinary professional. Called upon to serve the Goddess and execute Her mission, Miriam had committed herself to the enhancement of feminine beauty. Consumed by a sense of service, a Goddess worshipper, Miriam's attitude to her work was, in fact, driven. Miriam was possessed, fueled by psychic values that belonged in the Goddess' sensual realm. Her exuberant dedication reflected an absolute certainty, the sort of exclusiveness which revealed a state of identification with archetypal impersonal contents, rather than with a spontaneous individual relatedness to her various customers.

[39]

An inversion within the monotheistic framework, an *enantiodromia* has occurred with Miriam. The Goddess seized her, causing a one-sided inflation. Feminine archetypal contents were what Miriam lived out. An inflation steered her into a compulsive way of being that she could not stop; it was her mission. Miriam acted as a dispenser of the Goddess, Her evangelist. In her salon, ancient rites concerning feminine beauty reassumed ritualistic dimensions. A sacred air permeated each appointment, transposing regular customers into the elevated status of temple initiates.

Miriam was a *psychopomp*, a guide for sublime cause, a zealous mentor, instructing her clients diligently on their respective assignments to improve their appearance. In the field of contemporary cosmetics Miriam excelled, a skilled master of her art. A witch, a magician, Miriam superbly mixed various potions.

Miriam's lips were sealed about her professional secrets. Shrewd, witty, a superb businesswoman, Miriam tended skillfully to her income, to reaping her well-earned rewards. Resourceful, connected to her earthly instincts, Miriam seemed fulfilled. She did not have to pretend happiness; she was indeed self-realized. Our first appointment commenced a beneficial mentor-apprentice dialogue for the two of us. I found "feminine" wisdom in Miriam. Confident in her abilities, this unfailing devotee of the Goddess provided me with steadfast guidance into the realm of the senses.

A Tormented Hero

><del>◄━►</del>

Come taste our kisses... soft caresses shall
calm your yearnings.[4]

THE THIRD event followed in rapid succession. The night after my New York appointment with Miriam, I attended a performance of "Tannhäuser." From the Metropolitan Opera House stage, themes of feminine erotic-sensuality called out to me.

Unlike the two preceding episodes, which involved me personally, here was a dramatic presentation of erotic sensuality. However, by no means did I find the opera an objective presentation of its subject matter. Richard Wagner was a rebel who dared to explore such dangerous topics as erotic-sensual psychic energy. He was still, nevertheless, a prisoner of his biased period, chained to Christian dogmas. So, Wagner was split. The libretto treats the erotic-sensual realm one-sidedly, as a negative possession that is exclusively destructive. In contrast, the music succeeds in conveying both his admiration for, and attraction to, the primeval elemental powers of erotic-sensuality. Thus, whenever the opera is discussed in this context, it is focused on the libretto. The music compensates for this one-sided, intolerant attitude of the libretto, and succeeds in portraying Wagner's vision of erotic-sensuality as sublime, fascinating, and elating. Thus it is

---

[4]Richard Wagner, "Tannhäuser," libretto.

only Wagner's official credo, the "manifested," acknowledgment implying that erotic-sensual energies are of no positive value and of little merit. The "latent" attitude, to which Wagner could not openly admit, was a loud "Amen" to the numinosity of the erotic-sensual realm. In the arena of the opera, Wagner's divine music ultimately expresses his profound beliefs.

The hero, Tannhäuser, reflects the dichotomy between spirit/flesh or virgin/whore, a traditional split perceived as a war waged between good/evil polarities. Psychologically, the opposites mirror two halves, which together represent a whole. Psychic reality is founded in the coexistence of opposites rather than on an either/or existence. Instead of reconciling the opposites, Christian ethical values perpetuated a one-dimensional split.

Even though Wagner represents a pagan erotic-sensual realm as irresistible, its essence is interpreted as shadowy. Implicitly it amounts to the domain of the devil since human souls are inevitably ruined there. In contrast, the righteous intentionality of Christian morality is embedded in noble desires to guide human souls to immortality.

Thus, the official manifesto, the given system of beliefs that directs the opera's libretto, warns against feminine erotic-sensual powers as a pagan evil course that leads to Hell. In contrast, Christian values constitute a path to eternal Heaven.

These Christian axiomatic tenets present a deterministic doctrine that leaves humans no free choice. The consequences of human actions yield mechanistic either/or extreme results, polarized into salvation or doom. Fate is sealed *a priori*, in accordance with reward or punishment for inclinations or movements. Tendencies which pull in the direction of erotic-sensuality are automatically defined as sinful. Moreover, such attractions can only be interpreted as caused by "lower" powers—a spell or bewitchment—psychologically defined as overwhelming unconscious powers that defeat the ego by silencing its capacity to judge reality correctly, which bring about irresistible temptations, stemming from primitive instincts. Such temptations inevitably lead to great disasters.

Tannhäuser, a medieval minstrel, oscillates between these realms, embodied by the Goddess Venus as against Elisabeth, a value carrier of the Virgin Mary. His instincts draw him toward Venus, who is depicted as a seductive and devouring entity, an inescapable trap for humans. Tannhäuser, consumed by passion for the voluptuous Goddess, is being toyed with, prey to Venus' merciless manipulations.

After reveling with Venus, Tannhäuser returns to the place where a strict Christian ethic governs his mind and duties. At home, Elisabeth, a chaste, immaculate maiden, the epitome of purity and devotion, is waiting patiently for the return of her love. The antithesis to the ruthless Venus, Elisabeth loves Tannhäuser unconditionally.

Later, in the midst of a minstrels' gathering, during a singing competition, Tannhäuser is again seized by a greater power and goes into a trance. Uncontrollably, he sings an impassioned praise to Venus. This action instantly shifts his position to that of an accursed, defenseless man since he has broken all rules. Elisabeth's love can no longer protect the erring mortal.

Seeking expiation for his sins through papal absolution, Tannhäuser embarks on a pilgrimage to Rome where he is rejected and declared an eternal outcast. The Wagnerian hero is destined to be dismembered for his lust, torn asunder by the conflict, and punished.

When Elisabeth kills herself, Tannhäuser's curse is redeemed. His soul is saved. Her intervention is a Christian triumph, earning her lover, at his death, everlasting life. "Two souls have entered Heaven together," is the chorus' final song.

I thought over two matters, as I left the performance. First, mortals cannot relate directly to deities. A deity is an archetype. Human eros becomes an impossibility with God, since it is an archetypal non-relatedness. Direct human contact with a deity brings about a lethal state of possession by archetypal contents. Invaded, humans are lost, destroyed. Love with a deity is unsafe. Unthreatened, protected love can evolve only when archetypal contents are mitigated; human mediation mitigates pure archetype. Love requires two human mortals. The sensual realm of the opera is an *a priori* impossibility since Venus, being an unequal eros partner, cannot be related to directly by a mortal man. Tannhäuser's state of being overwhelmed is a direct consequence of the divine energies Venus incarnates and projects. In contrast, Elisabeth, who is a mortal woman, is an eros partner, with whom a love relationship is possible. Thus, in principle, the two realms, erotic-sensuality versus Christian ethics, as presented in the opera, do not offer equal partnership.

Secondly, I was struck by an indirect affirmation of life's instinctual sensuality, its autonomous growth and change, as expressed by Wagner's symbolic representation of the Pope's staff. Tannhäuser's repentance was to be accepted, according to the opera's libretto, in the impossible event that the Pope's staff grows leaves. Lo and behold, miraculously, the staff has green leaves. This living declaration is a credo to life's transcendent vigor, indirectly a triumph of the realm of sensuous passions. In spite of the Pope's harsh treatment of the sensual realm, the dynamic expression of life's passionate exuberance was affirmed and implied in this particular symbol, the greening of the staff. It conveys Wagner's latent message, his faith in instinctual life.

Apparently Wagner's times were still restricted by theological dogma and convention. It was historically premature, during Wagner's lifetime, to wrestle with issues of an apt reconciliation of "spirit/flesh" feminine psychic energies—meaning the relatedness of spirituality and sensuality. Wagner's preoccupation with the erotic-sensual feminine domain raised the question, however, although rapprochement between sensuality and spirit was beyond him. A redemption of sensuality, an acknowledgment of its sacred divinity, could not have been boldly declared in his time. This rapprochement is more likely to be a current enterprise, a task worthy of our endeavors. We are called upon to redeem the sensual realm. It is an appropriate opus for our time.

Through Tannhäuser, I was once more compelled to reflect on erotic-sensuality, this time within an historical-theological perspective.

Ambivalence: A Restrained Redemption of Feminine Erotic Sensuality

——◆——

The land of my soul is mine alone. Even as I draw
back, I move forward in the solitude of my soul.[5]

SALLY has been in analysis with me for over a year. She, too, contributed unknowingly to the events that took place during the same Epiphany week by bringing three consecutive dreams. I witnessed, vicariously, her encounter with the erotic-sensual domain. I also knew her dreams carried meaning for me. Sally's dream became the fourth event that week.

Raised in a Midwestern upper-class home near Chicago, Sally attended excellent preparatory schools and attained a Ph.D. For many years before I met her she taught literature in a prestigious women's college. Proud, self-sufficient, her persona intact, few, if any, would suspect her profound anguish or notice her frequent depressions. Behind it, well hidden, a deep rage consumed Sally, taking an indirect form, only acknowledged by her as poor health. She could not admit to more than physical symptoms. Poor health finally drove her to seek therapy, not out of faith, but as a last resort. Crippling allergies prevented her engagement in the outer world. As the allergies worsened progressively, her reality became restricted and greatly impoverished.

---

[5]Marc Chagall in a 1976 TV interview.

In clinical terms, Sally suffered a severe neurosis. A tyranni-
cal superego pushed ahead its insidious control, manifested
through a progressive interference with life's spontaneous flow of
events and activities. Judged harshly from within, Sally incorporated prohibitions and punishments, particularly in relationship
to her intimate erotic-sensual femininity. This could be inferred
from her life history and the ongoing experiences shared in her
analytical sessions, accompanied by her dreams.

Etiologically psychic inhibitions and repressions sabotaged
Sally's contact with the instinctual-sensual matrix. She was aware
of, and restricted by, severe psychosomatic symptoms which perpetuated and legitimized her increasing isolation. Sally's allergies
conveyed an objection, a resistance to life's pulsating dynamics.
Psychic movement toward growth, flourishing, vigor, primal
strivings, opening up to the exciting and unknown, all of these
were strictly forbidden. All that pleases humans as they gladly
expose themselves to seasonal changes proved aggravating for
Sally's health condition. Fierce allergies were Sally's somatic
response, devouring her physical and mental state. In particular,
Spring was her enemy. In her conversations, Sally identified flow-
ers, scents, bushes, and trees in bloom as her main adversaries.

Sally desired to halt Spring, as well as Summer. Everyone else
yearned for the arrival of warmth after the harsh Winter. Sally
dreaded being sick. How she wished she could control the seasons, since her emotional misery was converted to an unbearable
concrete literal misery, a total imprisonment, especially during
these seasons.

When I began to work with Sally, she was busy slowing life's
pulse by hiding behind poor health. She was forced to narrow
down and eliminate most activities. Confined, she lived in sheer
agony. Still, the alternative, to be flowing with life, sensually

engaged, to confront desires, was even more frightening. However, holding on to the status quo brought no relief.

Upon coming to therapy, Sally insisted politely, but firmly, that I remove all my plants and flower vases from my study before each session, not to mention requesting that I refrain from lighting candles which I was fond of doing. These demands symbolized Sally's desire that I merge with her and participate in her suffering and restrictions. I elected to cooperate with her requests. I realized that these were no mere whims. In an unconscious anticipation, I was to become an inseparable part of her imposed limitations. A representative of life's flow, I was invited, or better still, forced, to take part in Sally's gloomy perspective, not just symbolically, as most analysands expect of the analyst, but rather concretely. This literal identification, a merging, can be a criterion for the analysand's regression into a borderline state. Such analysands refuse to respect and accept boundaries.

Next came Sally's endless complaints, targeted mainly at me, my shortcomings, my incapacity to comprehend or to help. We both had to persevere in enduring an autonomous superego, a harsh judge who obsessively criticized us both. At the beginning of our work, I was forced to endure the incessant toxicity which engulfed Sally at all times.

Nevertheless, Sally seemed to be blessed in her analytical work, graced with an autonomous unconscious vitality. A steady flow of dreams guided the psychic process, presenting a compensatory active contrast to her dull, immobilized waking life. It was remarkable to witness the vigor of her unconscious, directed at restoring Sally's psychic balance and, consequently, her health. I found this psychic cooperation extraordinary and rejoiced for Sally.

Consequently, even though Sally's compulsive negativity went on for quite some time, her physical state improved steadily. She began to go out, meet with friends and attend social gatherings, in particular lectures and workshops.

Synchronicity was apparent as she brought the following dreams, as if a manifestation of my own inner pace. In essence, manifestations are central to the nature of the Epiphany week. By manifesting themselves, events assume a credible reality, meriting attention. Sally's three dreams elected to present her most neglected and dreaded subject matter, namely, erotic-sensual themes. I found Sally's ultimate encounter with her repressed sensuality more than a mere coincidence with my own quest. The synchronistic timing amazed me.

Of the three consecutive dreams that emerged, only the first two were interpreted. The third one was too explicit for Sally's fragile adaptation and she simply denied ever having dreamed it. Sally narrated the first dream.

> *I am sitting in an office, writing my doctoral thesis. The building is surrounded by an exquisitely blooming garden. Suddenly I become aware that a small statue of Aphrodite is awaiting me in the garden. Never having seen it before, I just know that it is my duty, an inner Call, to recover the statue. It feels like a command which I must obey. Without caution, with no delay or uncertainty, I get up and descend into the garden which had been a strictly forbidden zone until now, since my allergies tend to flare up as soon as I enter a similar environment. Among heavily scented flowers and thick growth of bushes, I indeed discover a fine, dainty statue of Aphrodite. To my surprise, instead of getting sick,*

> *I collect the statue calmly and proceed to carry it into*
> *my living quarters.*

Aphrodite, the Goddess of erotic sensuality, reappears in Sally's next dream, which occurred two nights later. In the second dream the sensual themes are much more bold, this time relating directly to Sally's sexuality as expressed in her marital life.

> *It is nighttime in our bedroom. I look around and*
> *notice a photograph of Aphrodite on the wall. We are*
> *in bed. Over the years, until now it has been my cus-*
> *tom to never initiate sex. Rather, I used to remain pas-*
> *sive, waiting for my husband to approach me. I was*
> *forbidden, from within, to express sexual desires.*
> *Unexpectedly, it becomes clear to me that to declare my*
> *sensual wishes is my birthright, equal to my husband's,*
> *that I am allowed to commence love-making when I*
> *crave sex. For the first time in my life I know, a deep*
> *knowledge, that I deserve to express my eroticism. So*
> *I initiate the intimacy with my husband and realize*
> *with pleasure that I have just inaugurated a new*
> *phase, courageously true to myself. I am no longer shy*
> *about my "animal" lust.*

In the first dream, Sally entered the forbidden garden, itself a sensual-erotic symbol, and found—in the midst of this danger—a potential for passion. (Actually, it is in these frightening and dangerous areas the treasure is generally found.) Instead of becoming sick upon encountering the blooming garden, it was the promise of sensual love, a healing potential represented by the statue of Aphrodite that Sally discovered. Aphrodite symbolizes sensual love. The statue of Aphrodite, a symbol of erotic-sensual freedom, is given to Sally to "carry home" in order to relate to the experience consciously. However, Aphrodite, being a statue in the first dream, was still a "safe" and quite impersonal symbol, so Sally could cope successfully with its erotic-sensual contents. In contrast, she was greatly alarmed by her second dream, her "bedroom dream." It carried too explicit a message. Sally became frightened and anxious at the prospect of "wildly" expressing and unleashing her deprived erotic-sensuality. Unable to admit her starved sexuality, it still seemed shameful and primitive to her sensibilities.

Sally's psyche was racing fast, too rapidly for her fragile ego. Repressed, cut off from her instincts for many years, Sally experienced an immense threat to her delicate balance. Subsequently, Sally totally denied having had a third dream, a dream which was shared with me in the previous session. In fact, it is rare and most unusual in a course of therapy for one to take back a dream which did occur and pretend it never did. Sally actually told me that such a dream had never taken place. What is indicated when such a phenomenon appears is how dangerous it must be for the dreamer to embrace the dream contents consciously, how impossible as of yet. Thus the fierce denials were a desperate defense mechanism, since the benefit of denial is a distortion of reality. No wonder the message of the dream proved too candid for Sally.

I teach prostitution at the college.

Sally could not accept yet the fact that dreams are to be treated symbolically and not to be taken literally. Her profound guilt in regard to erotic-sensual desires was too overwhelming, her shame at admitting sexual lust too great.

At this early phase of our analytical work together I decided to collude with Sally's denial. Much later in the treatment, elucidation of such an episode could come up and Sally's capacity to admit to human needs and even be accountable for these could become solid. The unconscious tends to repeat significant themes; thus with no pressure, no coercing of premature interpretations, inner maturation processes allow the transformation required to accept "shadowy," until-now, matters. They lose their *tremendum*, their terrifying hold, their "devilish" numinous qualities. Sally's therapy progressed steadily. A year later, her health improved, Sally once more participated in life's activities. Of course, she was much more pleasant to be around. People and relationships came her way.

Dawn

Oh my lady
my queen
I unfold your splendor in all lands
I extol your glory
I will praise your course
your sweeping grandeur
forever

   . . .

Queen
Mistress
You are sublime
You are venerable
Your great deeds
are boundless
May I praise
Your eminence
sweet is your praise

   . . .

Who can match your divinity
Who can match your rites

   . . .

Who spread over the land
the splendid brilliance of your divinity?[6]

---

[6]"Lady of the Largest Heart" in *Uncursing the Dark* is a rendition by Betty Meador of the Temple Hymn to Sumerian Goddess Inanna, written by her High Priestess, Enheduanna, 4300 years ago (Wilmette, IL: Chiron, 1992), p. 136. Used by kind permission.

FINALLY it became my turn. Four events, four times, a quaternity was completed as the Epiphany week church bells stopped ringing. The numinous week came to a close and so did my task, my awakening.

Each episode, though presenting itself independently, became interconnected in my psyche. Psychic processes have their own logic, gathering *prima materia* from various accessible sources in order to gather momentum and acquire conscious meaning. I was being asked to explore feminine erotic-sensual themes. My soul determined on an *enantiodromia*, a compensatory psychic movement. I was invited to relate to sensual femininity and consciously illuminate my findings.

This belated return to feminine roots has come as a blessing, a release from a state of captivity and imprisonment by masculine values. My fate had been characteristic, no different from that of most women. Severed from their earthly femaleness, their sensuality had remained split-off, alien, unconscious.

I was not asked to renounce my monotheistic roots, to abnegate my spiritual heritage whose values the feminine has incorporated beneficially in the last two millennia. The task was, rather, to consciously integrate archetypal erotic-sensual energies. My modern psyche called for a symbolic adaptation of ancient psychic contents. I was not directed toward simplistic concrete imitations of a primeval Goddess. I was called instead to invoke an attitude of reverence, an honoring of sacred feminine values. This attitude of reverence was an honoring of one of the Goddess' divine aspects—Her earthly erotic-sensual powers.

CHAPTER THREE

Unbound from the Past

Gleaning: Is Anyone There?

—◆—

Woman, know thyself.[1]

*And who knoweth whether thou art come to the
kingdom for such a time as this?*

—(ESTHER 4:14)

THERE are no ordinary analytic
sessions. Each hour takes on a life of its own: hence its unique-
ness. Nevertheless, for all analysts, certain analytical hours stand
out, a treasure to behold and remember. I often contemplate the
incomprehensible source of such hours. This wondrousness, I
came to believe, is rooted in a state of grace. A transcendent spirit hovers over these encounters. We analysts are then reminded
that we are engaged in a vocation, not merely a profession. The
autonomy of the psyche is revealed in all its splendor on these
occasions, and the two participants (and witnesses), analyst and
analysand, emerge transformed. Surely "for such times" as these
we did "come to the kingdom."

> *In the Garden of Eden The Lord God called unto
> Adam, and said unto him, "Where art thou?"
> (Genesis 3:9). The all-knowing God knew Adam's*

---

[1]Apollo's command as inscribed in this temple. Paraphrased.

*whereabouts. Instead, it was Adam who had to become
aware of his identity.*

—(HASSIDIC TALE)

Sharon, a journalist in her mid-30s, had been depressed and immobilized for several weeks. A few months into her analytical work, Sharon stormed into my office. Woken up by sheer fury, she arrived at the session incensed, enraged, agitated. "I loathe driving for hours in order to be engaged in a vague, pretentious project labeled 'healing,'" Sharon exclaimed contemptuously. "With endless support groups, weekend retreats, workshops, and, worst of all, this Jungian analysis, I despise this grand deceit. What a waste! What a bore it all is! I hate it!"

Sarcasm, irony, cynicism, sneering, ridiculing, smart-aleckness, sardonic grins, caustic remarks, all belonged to Sharon's rich arsenal during the initial period of analysis. Intelligent and sophisticated, Sharon had sharpened and perfected these characteristic tools to convey her embittered disillusionment. This arsenal was designed to hide her pain. All these defense mechanisms were intended to conceal the fact that Sharon was in the midst of an acute crisis. It took her several months to peel off the defenses and expose to herself (and to me) her bleak reality. Then she began to face courageously her distress, her sense of despondency, her excruciating heartache, and to confess her collapse.

The anguish and the profound sorrow are inevitable companions of all who embark on psychic transitions. Sharon left a prestigious marriage, financial security, respectable social status. All were gone! When the previous stormy phase had ended, the distractions based on righteous convictions ceased, the fierce accusations and mutual blamings stopped, the war was over. Sharon was left with the knowledge of a wretched defeat. There was no peace in the stillness around her, only a dreadful vacancy, a sense of nothingness. "Blankness! Silence," she commented, smiling resentfully, "just for starters."

Sharon's vitality was gone, consumed in an infinite void. Her loneliness swept her into profound despair, and mocked her foolishness, her stupidity. Torn by grief, Sharon was devoured by ambiguities in regard to her fateful decision. Enveloped by melancholy, in the grip of bottomless desolation, relentless ruminations tortured her endlessly, reprimanding Sharon for this mistaken irreversible course of action she had taken. The taunting echoes repeated the same unanswerable questions: "Who am I? Is there anyone there?"

Worst of all, a crescendo of inner voices persecuted Sharon, accusing her harshly: "You are to blame! It is all your fault! What a blunder." The voices laughed, attacking her at unexpected times. They hit at her again and again in whispering, screaming, yelling, shrieking tones. Later, the insults increased, spraying their venom: "You scum of the earth, who will ever want you?"

The voices viciously scorned Sharon's femininity, her "cheap nature, her whorelike sleaziness." Sensual demeanor, erotic attractiveness, sexual desires, all were degraded, held in contempt. The voices humiliated Sharon, further injuring her remaining shreds of self-worth, fueling her unbearable self-hatred. The constant, stubborn raids by the inner voices, the loud abusive put-downs, the pounding judgments, destroyed her. Prey to misgivings and regrets, she felt so weakened that she wished to sink into oblivion and die.

As an analyst, I was privileged to have witnessed all of this suffering many times before, always attempting to provide a solid vessel to contain the erupting "disintegration" which commonly seized women forced to undergo psychic transformations.

Sharon, a novice in this arena, could not have an appreciation for the positive meaning behind her despair. She had no idea that the latter served as the psychic mover, designed in order ultimately to lead her onto a new path.

Sharon could not possibly know as of yet that her inevitable fall into the abyss of depression was, in fact, an initiatory process from which she would finally emerge transformed. Her darkness signified the partaking of a descent into the unconscious, a Nekiyah ritual whose purpose meant entering a gateway into a new phase. Finally, Sharon's pain had to be understood as analo-gous to a mourner's lament at a funeral, a clinging to the past, a yearning to view it in all its glory, identifying one-sidedly with the previous course, forgetting that the essence of death is rebirth.

Still an outsider, Sharon lived out an alien psychic reality, not realizing that she had stepped into a brand new terrain. It felt foreign—an enigma. No one freely volunteers for the tasks Sharon faced, yet many women have dared parallel encounters. Women often take part in a feminine destiny whose auto-nomous *teleos*, its higher purpose, eludes the voluntary will power of each participant.

Why, on this morning, was I so unexpectedly moved, touched to the core of my being, by Sharon's grief? Her help-lessness, her hopelessness, why did they affect me so, her cries piercing my heart, penetrating far beyond the surface layers of an "analytical stance?"

My vocation had always provided me with the tools to adhere to the role of midwife, to endure my analysand's labor pains. Why did my lengthy experience fail me at this very hour? Why did the clinical terms seem ridiculous now? The earned authority to serve "maturation processes" disappeared, the mastering of an "impartial objectivity" vanished, the acquired demeanor of a "participant observer" deserted me. Why did these various highly cultivated skills simply cease to exist at this time?

The only explanation that seems valid for me is that a state of grace replaced mundane skills. This was one of these hours, "Such time for which we come to the kingdom," when God enters and intervenes, choosing our words for us. Unannounced, all of a sudden, I was compelled to grow, shocked into an awakening. I became Adam, summoned by God to discover my whereabouts. Sharon's crisis stirred up my crisis. Her dread mirrored my own, serving my opportune psychic transformation. The clinical term "countertransference" does no justice to that psychic reality.

The moment an analysand constellates the analyst's unconscious, the analyst faces an inner task, a dialogue with a greater authority within herself. The analyst's response to the analysand during "such a time," even though assuming a spontaneous shape, emerges from a deep psychic layer and is endowed with an autonomous Self quality. The response is indeed directed at the analyst, at furthering her self-awareness. I trusted the independent source which directed my words. I found myself telling Sharon: "Perhaps all your psychic endeavors are harnessed in the service of gleaning. During life's great transitions, everyone is incapable of nurturing herself for a while. At this period of your life you are being directed to glean. . . ."

I recall pondering my use of the unusual word "glean," puzzled by the rare expression which was not planned by my ego. Beyond its literal meaning "to gather, to collect, to harvest," gleaning is reserved for the biblical Book of Ruth which is suffused with such radiant values as devotion, love, compassion, tolerance and loyalty. When did I become a modern-day Naomi?

"Let me now go to the field, and glean. . . ." (Ruth 2:2). I knew the word was chosen by my psyche. "To glean" is not simply a word, it is a symbol of the gentle caring that Ruth's myth connotes. Eros is the myth's evangelion.

"Please acknowledge your gleaning rights as a foreigner. On your sojurn you are a mere novice, a newcomer, in an unfamiliar land," I said to Sharon. "Recognize yourself as such and take full advantage of your present limitations. Allow yourself to receive and harvest as much as you can: our analytical work, your dreams, the various workshops, the weekend retreats you attend. Collect and gather it all, an abundance offered you at this time. Permit yourself to be nurtured by others for this time, until you are no longer an outsider, until you arrive at that which you can call your own home."

These reassuring comments became a source of comfort for Sharon. Relieved temporarily, she regained her composure and calmly proceeded to discuss current issues. A transient relief is the very best one could hope for in a morning session with a woman in Sharon's predicament. An ephemeral calm was the gift given her at this graced hour. For me the last exchange during the session marked a commencement. In meditating upon the Book of Ruth, I was inspired to begin a search for the myth's living meaning today. By studying Ruth's ways and allowing a conscious integration of the psychic values represented by her I was guided to trust that modern-day "foreigners," women who engage in psychic transitions, can be loved and cared for like Ruth. Like Ruth, they deserve an emotional security while on their destined journeys. I proceeded to record these ideas.

What Ails My Women Analysands: The Loss of the Goddess' Sacred Vulva

—◄◆►—

*I find myself at the bottom of the ocean. Then I hear
a female voice saying to me: Look at yourself and
you shall see me. Look at yourself forever.*[2]

*I believe only in the Word become flesh,
in the spirit filled body.*[3]

WHAT ails my women analysands?
In describing the vocational aspects of my analysands, the phrase
"a good adaptation" would be an appropriate term. Bright,
accomplished in their respective professions, the workplace has
been, for the majority of my analysands, an area of resourcefulness and capability.

My analysands attain fulfillment in the area that had previ-
ously been an exclusive masculine domain during two millennia
of monotheistic reign, and, simultaneously, the workplace is the
site of their greatest defeat. Namely, an ironic and cruel paradox
determines my analysands' self-worth, for they rely upon masculine premises which derive from masculine attitudes and values.
The latter do not furnish a solid foundation for women's well-
being. The analysands' success at work contributes to a one-sided,
impersonal mode of living, ruled only by ideas and principles.

---

[2] An excerpt from active imagination from Dorothy, an analysand.
[3] C. G. Jung, *Collected Works,* vol. 10, ¶917.

So, what went wrong? Why are my women analysands so upset, unhappy, and fragile? Why is it that these assertive personas, exuding confidence, conceal "little girls" who are desperately endeavoring to hide their psychic reality—an agitated woundedness—violated, ill-treated, brittle, defenseless, and unprotected. An impressive facade is no substitute for a solid sense of ego identity. In fact, their bewilderment is augmented by the current pressure from feminist ideology (which itself lacks solid roots in the feminine) to shift their loyalty away from their traditional patriarchal adaptation which is based upon masculine values. Unintentionally, early feminism issued illusory recommendations that caused damage and turmoil.

My analysands to do not have an inner groundedness that is adequate. This groundedness is required in order to genuinely execute the collective feminist demand, which doesn't yet offer real guidance in the process of developing the feminine. The feminist movement still seems to rely on superficial changes. Having never evolved an inner connection their feminine core, ungrounded in their own feminine instinctual matrix, they lead an unstable existence, haunted by anxieties, depressions, panic attacks.

Many of my analysands are alienated from the archetypal feminine center. This affliction has assailed womanhood for two millennia. However, the earlier alienation was inevitable, imposed on the feminine during the establishment of patriarchal sovereignty. Recently, however, the alienation has evolved into a voluntary animus imprisonment.

At the core of my women analysands' distress and anguish is, psychologically, an inner "man," or *animus*, in Jungian terms, which has surpassed its limits. Life is directed mainly by a masculine alignment. The early days of the women's movement promoted self-realization in masculine terms, thus initiating a competition with the masculine realm by imitating it. The agonizing injury caused by obeying these feminist guidelines became even more painful, since the obedience was prompted by a whole-hearted trust in an enlightened feminist sisterhood. Instead of relating to the "inner man" from a feminine center, my women analysands were seized by being "him" concretely. They were inflated by archetypal male contents that controlled their lives with an absolute certainty, characteristic of psychological states of possession.

The possession by masculine contents was perceived unconsciously as a hostile threat by my women analysands. In fact, their dreams indicated a danger to their feminine essence, symbolized by their female organs, as reflected by the following motif. Leah dreamed:

> *A male doctor is preparing a huge needle to inject into my breast. He intends to insert metal cylinders into my uterus. I am terrified.*

A common feature of all these women is their sense of the void, of uprootedness, of an estrangement from an autonomous instinctual female base. One of my analysands expressed it succinctly when she said, pondering aloud her situation, "I have spread my wings although I have no roots, after all is said and done." Another woman analysand tells her analyst. "I have grown up cut off at the ankles from earth."[4] In fact, professional status and societal influences often seem hollow and elusive without an inner connection to an innate feminine nature. My women analysands were powerless to make free choices. They were not free to be themselves.

---

[4] Sylvia Brinton Perera, *Descent to the Goddess* (Toronto: Inner City Books, 1981), p. 7

The distortion in modern identity was mirrored in the consultation room: sad, unhappy, lonely, all these women shared a profound sense of mourning. What part of their being was not alive? Is it an outer or inner place that they grieve for? They all mourned the loss of Eros' capacity, the ability to develop inner and outer relationships from their hearts. They had lost an innate instinctual mentorship, an inherent guidance to act in accordance with their feelings.

This loss is why the soul, the feminine soul, has gone away. In the sessions my analysands wept, they cried out, they longed for a "non-presence," their souls. The much larger question behind the individual abandoned Eros-relatedness of my analysands is the neglect of female divinity, a betrayal of erotic-sensual psychic energies symbolized by the Goddess' sacred vulva. The divinity of the archetypal feminine, transpersonal psychic layers, the source of innate female power and instinctual wisdom, has been severed from contemporary feminine consciousness.

The sacred vulva lends support to feminine groundedness in women's instincts and feelings, a sense of dignified self-respect. A rejection of erotic-sensual energies by my modern analysands meant a rejection of the sacredness of the Goddess. Wounded little girls have no notion of the sacred vulva, their womanhood is thwarted.

The denial of their own sacredness leaves my women analysands troubled. Personally, without appropriate protection, they remain forever motherless orphans having never received a mother's true caring. Behind it, on a collective transpersonal level, the split from their instinctual divinity created an anguished misery. Anguish, sorrow, and pain are my analysands' symptoms.

Regaining the Goddess' Sacred Vulva through Dreamwork

———❖———

In habinetum symbolum facilior est transitus.
For those having the symbol, the transition is more
easily made.

—AN OLD ALCHEMICAL SAYING

With the honey and pleasure of the senses and the joy of
life . . . the healing and "whole-making" medicine, which
is recognized even by modern psychotherapy, is combined
with spiritual and conjugal love . . . the whole of the con-
scious man is surrendered to the self, to the new centre of
personality...[5]

Return often and take me
beloved sensation, return and take me...,
...my sensual life
how plainly I see their meaning there...
The joy and the essence of my life is the story
of the hours when I found and sustained sensual
delights as I desired it.[6]

---

[5] C. G. Jung. *Collected Works*, vol. 14, ¶704.
[6] C. P. Cavafy, "Return," "Understanding," "Sensual Delight" in *The Complete Poems of Cavafy,* Rae Dalven, ed. Copyright © 1961 and renewed 1987 by Rae Dalven. Reprinted by permission of Harcourt Brace & Company, Orlando, and Hogarth Press, London.

DREAM work has been the *via regia*, the bridge, the main channel to the rediscovery of repressed feminine erotic-sensual contents alive in the unconscious of my women analysands. Dream interpretation has proven a powerful tool, leading to a consistent path, to healing. Within this context healing means the capacity for psychic transformation through greater clarity and understanding. One understands the essence of the split-off unconscious material and consciously integrates this material.

Understanding dream messages that are transmitted in symbolic language is a difficult task. Honesty, patience, and the capacity to endure pain caused by startling discoveries are required. Self-discovery returns women analysands to their primary relatedness to erotic-sensual passions and to the archetypal feminine essence.

It is an exception when modern women are consciously aware of their erotic-sensual passions. Marianne's childhood recollections were such an exception. Marianne, a dentist, was brought up in a Catholic home and educated by strict nuns who preached at length against the "sins of the flesh." Yet, Marianne shared with me the following recollections: "I watched my budding breasts in the bathroom and could not wait to become a woman. These were the times when the atomic bomb hovered over us, threatening to explode. I was so sad to die young and thought to myself: "How terrible it would be to not ever delight in sexual pleasures."

The missing archetypal female matrix, a vital nurturing container, was conveyed through the dreams brought to the analytical work by the analysands. Dream images were discussed at length; their symbolic significance intended for the dreamer's awareness was deciphered.

The deep recesses of my women analysands' psyches were replete with exiled erotic-sensual and sexual themes. Manifold variations surrounded archetypal motifs of the harlot and the prostitute. Particular attention was devoted, while working through each dream, to the rediscovery of the primordial union that once existed in the remote past between erotic-sensual contents and the divinity attributed to them. In the past, this juxtaposition of sensual passion with religious numinosity constituted an elementary perception in the Goddess' cosmogony.

The degree of healing among my women analysands could be measured by the growing faith in the sacredness of the erotic psyche. Theirs was a progressive engagement in this feminine Opus of Redemption!

How then can the sacred vulva be regained by contemporary women if we are afraid to mention the word?

My women analysands brought dream images that combined sensual passion with the numinous religiosity. These dream images echo the original union that prevailed in ancient feminine cosmogony through the experience of the Goddess' sacred vulva. The sacred priestess, who carried human values for the Goddess, Her archetypal mediator, dispensed her secrets to mortals, and this image emerges in the dreams, as well.

Working through many dreams, women analysands embraced and consciously assimilated the life-affirming dream images. Erotic-sensual contents constituted an innate transpersonal aspect in each psyche. Slowly, women analysands learned to joyfully accept the erotic psyche as an innate part that anchors their personal reality to mature womanhood. They no longer led the lives of injured little girls, no longer were confused about their identity. During the analytical process, my women analysands learned to anticipate the erotic-sensual dream motifs from which they have been severed in waking life. They reached an understanding that the Goddess is an integral part of a modern-day Supreme Deity, or the Self. That understanding implies a sanctification of feminine erotic-sensual psychic energies, acknowledgment reached through emotional personal experiences rather than through abstract ideological principles. So, it is mainly dreamwork that healed my women analysands. Analysis is always a slow process and is an excellent environment in which to work through topos such as erotic-sensuality. The present generation is still heir to profound biases and prejudices. The contemporary shifts of archetypal energy from the masculine structure to the feminine create and shape both the collective and the individual directions of women. It is a slow change, for women are still heir to profound bias, a consequence of introjected monotheistic values.

A trusting surrender to life's mysteries has been required by my women analysands so that they can become grounded in their feminine roots, dignified initiates in this meaningful transformation.

Hilary, an analysand who worked as a scientist, was unaware of the Eleusinian Mysteries, the feminine religious initiation rituals held annually, the most revered event in ancient Greece. Yet her dream replicated exact details of the Eleusinian rituals.

> *An anonymous female voice of someone who loves me instructs me to put my hand into a dark basket. I obey, reach into the depth, and suddenly my hand is seized by snakes pulling my arm lower and lower. I am surprised at how calm I remain.*

Hilary's dream makes her a participant in the Eleusinian Mysteries whose meaning was a descent into the depths where the secrets of life and death are to be revealed.

Thelma's dream had a parallel "descent" intentionality. Unlike Hilary, Thelma descended using modern-day images. Thelma, a physiotherapist, described the dream.

> *Suddenly my eyeglasses fall down. As if they have a will of their own, the glasses roll downwards. In chasing them, I discover, beneath, lower floors, one built on top of the other. Finally my eyeglasses stop at the bottom, a very primitive basement.*

Thelma commented: "I comprehend the purpose for the eyeglasses' autonomous fall: I was to find out about the manifold levels of my underground floors, about their depth, which reveals their antiquity." Psychologically, Thelma is led back in time, descending into the depths, in order to reconnect with severed psychic contents. Thelma said: "Aided by the magnifying glasses, I was better capable of discerning the expanded sights, the lower floors, as well as acquiring a discerning insight into their inner meaning, namely a necessity to consciously expand and integrate ancient primitive contents that proved to be parts of my 'house'—meaning my psyche."

The unconscious is often teleological, purposeful. For example, Hilary and Thelma's two dreams aim at reconnection to ancient psychological roots, reflected in the "old wings" in Thelma's own house, and the access to Hilary's immemorial initiation rites.

Most commonly, the analysands' dreams simply revealed the split-off presence of female erotic-sensual energies that were

alien to their consciousness. In our contemporary conceptual-
ization, the following dream is compensatory in nature. It complements the dreamer's intellectual adaptation. Rita is a journalist whose persona reflects her identification with a literary and
solemn self-image. She confessed feelings of shame and disgrace
at her dream. Rita had the following dream.

> I was about to exit a clothing store. Just as I was leav-
> ing, I noticed a shining crimson silk cape, decorated
> with bright feathers and glittering gems, hanging on the
> door. The red cape was "flashy," vain, loud, seductive.
> It created a whorish look. Totally astonished at myself,
> I could not take my eyes off the cape. I was suddenly
> keenly interested in purchasing the cape even though I
> had no idea when or where I would wear it.

Thus the dream introduced Rita to an archetypal "inner harlot,"
hidden behind her earnest demeanor.

A frank admission of their sexual lust by the unconscious of
my women analysands, seemed to open up only in later stages of
the analytical work. After gathering sufficient ego strength, they
encountered and delighted in erotic-sensuality, which has, until
recently, been an estranged, forbidden, and denigrated subject. It
is at this later stage that dreams can be confronted and evoke
frank discussions concerning "voluptuous lust and sexual engagement." Impersonal sexual activities were allowed and elected in
the unconscious, and these emerged in analysands' dreams.
However, the discussion of "sacred erotic-sensuality" as an archetypal feminine notion, central to the Goddess' cosmogony, is not
fully ready for conscious integration as of yet. This is especially
apparent at the beginning stages of the analytical work.

The following dreams share a common denominator: erot-ic-sexuality is favored within academic settings, demonstrating a compensatory psychic need in women who admire cerebral or abstract attainments in the Western world. Lisa, a senior student at a prestigious women's college, is an industrious, idealistic young woman, active in feminist causes. Lisa narrates her dream.

> *I am led by a guide on a tour. I observe two rows of women facing each other along two opposite walls. One row consists of college students like me. The opposite row is made up of professional prostitutes. Without a moment's hesitation, I choose to join the prostitutes' line.*

Lisa was conscious of the fact that she did not resist the allure-ment of the "wholly other" which the enigmatic realm of whoredom seemed to offer her. For Lisa, this realm symbolized "an excitement as against a boring regime of studies." Sally, a college professor that I mentioned earlier, had a bold dream that frightened her to such a degree she denied having ever dreamed it.

> *I teach prostitution at my college. I train prostitutes. I wake up in sheer horror.*

Sally was not yet ready to accept an archetypal perception that sexual divinity can be a sacred path, in accordance with the Goddess' mentorship.

And what of "new age" women? For me, the predicament of "new age women" is not rooted in the patriarchal value system. Their conflict comes from a tendency to become enveloped in an ungrounded spirituality. Psychologically, these women tend to deny shadow tendencies, identify with an undifferentiated "loving persona." They often despise primitive female sensuality. They feel that sexual engagements are crude and offensive to their refined spiritual nobility. They believe that primitive innate instincts can be ignored or, at least, overcome. These beliefs are a modern, but simplistic version of the battle between the "power of Light against Darkness" within a contemporary feminine generation.

Dreams convey compensatory messages to these women: they indeed can combine erotic-sensuality with spirituality. They are told by the dreams that they have to abide by such a union. Betty, a "new age" psychotherapist, is told by her dream that genuine healing integrates sensual attractiveness.

> *It is night time. I go back to my trustworthy healer, Terry, in order to reclaim my clothes, which had remained in her closet. I discover that my clothes are glamorous evening gowns. How paradoxical, to reclaim this dazzling wardrobe in Terry's humble closet, of all places.*

Gloria, a "new age" art therapist, was asked by the dream she brought to the session to question her convictions. She narrated this dream.

> *My Sufi guru says to me: "I cannot come to your room. It is untidy!" I know my room is very clean. However, in the corner, my vine is covered with dry raisins instead of ripe grapes, since I neglected to gather the grapes in time.*

Gloria commented, "Dionysus, the God of wine and intoxication is also the God of inspiration and prophecy. I think that my guru did not approve of my neglect of Dionysus' grapevine." Thus the dreamer herself understood why her guru did not approve of her mode of living when the spirit lacks bubbling inspiration.

Joanna, a young teacher, very romantic and quite repressed, has been working for two years in therapy. She brought the following dream.

> *My lover is chased by a group of men, apparently evil, as compared to his innocent values. As he is chased away, he passes me a note which I hide in my vagina. I choose the vagina as a hiding place because it is a part of my body where I feel a lot of power.*

Joanna was unaware of the archetypal symbol of the sacred vulva. Nevertheless, she reclaimed her innate power, her share in the sacred vulva. Healing the feminine is ultimately concerned with the dignity and sacredness of the Goddess' vulva.

CHAPTER FOUR

The Restoration of the Feminine
within Monotheism

The Massadah Dream:
Diagnosis of Feminine Collective Suicide

Thou hast visited me in the night.

—(PSALMS 17:3)

SARA is a social worker in New York City. Her homeland is Israel. She brought the following dream to the analytical session.

I belong to a commune, a sacred sisterhood order, whose site is on top of Massadah. An oath has been taken by each member of the commune, a vow of celibacy, abstinence from any sexual engagement.

I am returning from a certain journey, glad to be back home. Climbing to the mountaintop, I choose to take the winding path. I find myself in the company of an unknown man who is attracted to me and who continuously stares at my breasts. I feel repulsed and disgusted. A celibate woman, I devote myself exclusively to spiritual values and despise the fact that men are ruled by sexuality. For me, they seem "creaturely," at the mercy of their flesh. So here I find myself with a savage representative of the male gender, as compared with the sublime guidelines that direct our sisterhood.

> *I loathe my companion and feel uncomfortable, more-*
> *over annoyed, at the lusty glances focused on my*
> *breasts. All this time we climb up the mountain in*
> *silence.*

"Is it possible to dream of Massadah and remain emotionally remote?" pondered Sara aloud to herself, feigning indifference. Years ago, she had visited Massadah, as do most Israeli youth. Although I doubted Sara's nonchalant lack of associations, I had to respect her right not to discuss her dream..

Massadah is not merely a historical location. Its sacred numinosity lives on. Its renewed meaning for Israelis today is carried on within a tradition, always permeated by Massadah's spirit, in which various initiation rites for contemporary youth groups are celebrated on the summit of the mountain.

Massadah is a steep mesa in the Judean desert, overlooking the Dead Sea. King Herod built a winter palace for himself there, erecting a fortress completely inaccessible to hostile intruders. Later, during the Great Jewish War (circa A.D. 66), a large group of Hebrew religious zealots inhabited the entire mountaintop, establishing a stable commune which was surrounded for years by Roman legions. After years of living under siege conditions, the Romans ascended the mountain by constructing a huge ramp. Expecting an easy victory, they discovered all nine hundred inhabitants, adults and children, dead. The entire community committed suicide, determined to die rather than surrender to a fate of exile, slavery, and humiliation. The wholesale premeditated suicide became a symbol, affirming absolute religious devotion. Within the historical context, suicide was the lucid choice to maintain religious loyalty to the One masculine God, and to remain spiritually free against all odds, that made

Massadah's heroic opus meaningful to future generations. The mountain embodies persistent endurance, and represents values that are worth dying for. A tangible stronghold, Massadah represents loyalty, commitment, steadfastness.

Massadah has been elevated into a religious and national symbol of the triumph of spiritual convictions. The monotheistic ethos finds in Massadah its appropriate numinous myth. The central idea conveyed by Massadah's history is a message that God's Holiness is more important than human survival. Transcending survival for the sake of ideology was a novel idea in the evolution of consciousness. "Kiddush-HaShem" is the Hebrew expression for a sanctification of God, meaning that even when self-sacrifice is involved, "God is there." The transcendence of spiritual ideas over physical survival is a giant leap in human ethics.

Massadah connotes a significant development psychologically: an *opus contra naturam*, the supreme transcendence of the spirit over survival instincts. The victory of the human spirit over Nature represents a new masculine worldview contrary to the sovereign former worldview of the Goddess' feminine domain. Her realm was Nature. In Nature earthly survival is a basic instinct. We must survive above all else. Transcendent values, commands of a higher spirit, did not exist as yet within the Goddess' framework. Between the two cosmogonies, that of the Goddess, as opposed to that of the God, Massadah symbolized a watershed. The Goddess promoted survival, Earth being Her arena. The heavenly God evoked notions of the supremacy of transcendent spiritual values, an alien idea to the Goddess.

In Sara's dream, the celibate sisterhood connotes an animosity to Eros, a severance from erotic-sensual instincts. "Joining in the sisterhood" means an obedient adherence to monotheistic

Logos principles. The "sisterhood" addiction to the spirit, living "high" on Massadah, denies, betrays, and starves the female core. The "sisterhood" connotes an anti-life attitude, an antithesis to the innately feminine. Sara's dream seems to state that as long as the feminine elects to remain "celibate" on Massadah, a lofty monastery imbued with ungrounded masculine spiritual tenets, the feminine is doomed to sterile detachment from its roots.

In Sara's dream the symbol of the celibate sisterhood on the Massadah mountaintop reflects a dangerous tendency for the feminine essence. Understood symbolically, anti-life tendencies and celibacy exhibit a self-destructive suicidal attitude, parallel to the concrete suicide which is associated with Massadah. The lofty, noble masculine values are not suited for the feminine. They represent a pathological split of the feminine from its innate instinctual nature. The dream implies a modern-day self-deception by the feminine through a disregard of the feminine vital core.

Additionally, the dream images mirror a dynamic psychic reality where projections operate. Only when the projections are withdrawn in either gender is there hope for human equality and Eros relatedness. In the dream, the feminine shadow is projected onto "male beastly sexuality." The renunciation of active sexual engagement by the "celibate sisterhood" brings about the displacement and projection of their feminine erotic-sensuality which perceives primitive sexual lust in the savage males. True relatedness to the masculine is obviously an impossibility as long as the masculine is perceived as devoid of the capacity for feeling. The quality of an Eros relatedness is completely denied the masculine through hostile anticipation. An enraged unconscious complex, loaded with emotional intensity, as all complexes are, fuels a distortion of psychic and physical reality by the feminine.

Thus, the masculine is also dehumanized. Trust—the prerequisite for communication—is absent when denial and projection defense mechanisms are constellated. Identified with the monotheistic spirit, the feminine dream ego, personified by Sara and her celibate sisters, is inflated, possessed by masculine spiritual archetypes.

Sara's dream of Massadah formulates a collective diagnosis of a distinct modern-day femininity which, unconsciously, falls into an *enantiodromia*; that is, into its contrary oppositional values by adoring masculinity.

Massadah is a paradigm of masculine spiritual values. Through its extreme history it challenges the worth of the inherent feminine receptivity. When feminine erotic-sensuality is devalued and banished by the feminine women, the "celibate sisterhood" on Massadah, it indicates confusion and betrayal by modern-day women, a leaping over feminine participation in life's flow.

Psychologically, the celibate sisterhood is possessed by a masculine spirit. The self-denial is conveyed symbolically by the very suicidal, psychic energy that permeated the historical Massadah. The zealous extremes indicated by the "celibate sisterhood" connotes a state of bewitchment of contemporary feminine psyches caused by the supremacy of masculine values. This bewitchment is, of course, unconscious.

Sara's dream is the result of an inflation of the feminine by masculine monotheistic values connoting an unconscious collusion with unearthly, anti-life energies. All psychological inflations end in a catastrophic deflation. Sara's dream is a warning.

Safed Dream:
Prognosis of Contemporary Deliverance

◦◦◦

I will lift up mine eyes unto the hills,
from whence cometh my help.

—(PSALMS 121:1)

DORIT, a psychiatrist born and raised in Israel, has spent the last twenty years in New York City. Dorit frequently remarks, "I am not particularly attached to my homeland." I often ponder the naiveté or self-deception of this emphatic declaration. Coming from a psychiatrist, it is all the more startling. Conscious intentions have little power over the stubborn insistence of the unconscious, which pushes back to its original inscapes, the cradle of the symbolic life, a nurturing locale for our innermost images. At least, one could honestly admit to a conflictual state of being split between two countries—being torn apart. The psyche is anchored in our birthplace. Psychologically, this psychic reality has to be acknowledged and respected. Our homeland is our fate.

Dorit entered my office. She mentioned having a dream. "It was a remarkable dream," she commented, "but rather than exploring it now, I need to look at some other critical concerns." Still, before she left the consulting room, she casually narrated her dream.

I am a young soldier, taking part in a battle to liber-
ate Safed. As the dream commences, it is a known fact

[84]

*that we have already won. Even though the town is
ours, there is one remaining task, most dangerous. This
is how the dream begins.*

*I am assigned the role of searching for snipers. This
means clearing individual houses, entering foreign ter-
ritories all by myself. An encounter with snipers, expert
marksmen, skilled and well-concealed, is frightening. I
am at a distinct disadvantage. No laws or common
sense predictions can assist in anticipating potential
developments. Even experts are not protected, let alone
myself. An untrained novice, a single woman facing
true masters on her own. I feel lonely and brittle.*

*Suddenly, in a miraculous, unexplained turn of
events, help comes my way. On both sides of the street
assigned to me, I can see two rows of Arab women
standing. Each of them stands in front of a house, yet
they form even, united rows of solidarity. It is understood that if any of them nods her head, it connotes a
warning sign, meaning that there are snipers in "her"
house, the house behind her, and I am then to avoid
that house! The Arab women's presence is a great relief.
In fact, my confidence is totally restored. I am able to
proceed, to successfully complete my mission.*

Dorit mentioned that Safed, an Israeli town, was never visited by
her. I did not press Dorit further. In our next session, when she
declined to return to the previous week's material, I made a note
of Dorit's refraining from working on this particular dream. I
assessed the dream's stature, its dramatic scope, as a carrier of
transpersonal contents. I knew it as a religious numinous dream.
It remained untouched by the dreamer.

Dorit, the young Israeli soldier, personifies a contemporary feminine ego, groomed to abide by monotheistic masculine values. Spiritual ideals govern her attitudes and behavior. Compliant to patriarchal rules, her femininity is possessed by superior archetypal ethical principles that belong to the masculine realm. Dorit has learned obedience. Like most women, her individuality is masked by a polite persona which orders her to follow norms of being "a good daughter to the Father." Life is then directed by guidelines of "should" and "ought" and natural instinctuality is curbed. Challenges are responded to with an indiscriminate dictate to be "good," "cooperative," a regimented compliance. Maidenhood and protracted "maiden psychology" replace mature womanhood within the monotheistic Western framework. The maiden is an archetypal pattern of a one-sided identification with "goodness" and purity. She is an "innocent girl" with a developed cooperative persona. Cut off from female instincts, she has no ground upon which to discern whom to trust and not to trust. The denial of her shadow leads her to projection of her aggression on others and, actually to invoke it in them. Her ego has not introjected accountability for her deeds and desires. In the Western world, women were trained to remain maidens. Ultimately, at this maidenhood phase, the persona, Dorit's appropriate image, is identical to her ego.

Ungrounded in reality, since she is divorced from instinctual earthly femininity, Dorit remains defenseless, unprotected. Compelled to live out compliance to collective impersonal norms, she is merely "a soldier in the army," as symbolized by the dream.

Dorit is fighting, though, for her individuality. This dream conveys the difficulties and fears involved in the task of individuation. The "civilized" feminine ego long severed from its earth, instinctual roots, needs assistance by this instinctual primal energy in order to acquire psychic freedom, "liberation."

The dream's autonomous resolution comes as a surprise. An abundant grounded female energy is available, accessible in Dorit's unconscious, embodied by the Arab women who band together. These two living chains represent a firm stance. Silent, determined, arms crossed over chests, the women's posture implies a "no-nonsense" demeanor. For Israelis, Arab women carry the female psychic energy of great perseverance in the face of adversity. Taught early in life to accept the inevitable, they learn to fight fiercely when it is required. Basic survival is their business, groundedness and obeying innate instincts serve to defend basic existence. They are grounded through female instinctual energies.

In Jungian terms, "persona" means a "social identity," an "ideal image," propriety and good manners cultivated in Western civilization. Persona is a superfluous commodity for the Arab women, when survival is at stake. Appropriate manners are irrelevant at that level, when endurance and persistence are what matters. To indulge in the cultivation of persona is a superficial luxury Arab women can ill afford. Shrewd, intuitive, alert, unshakable, these women depend on their alliance with their shadow. The shadow consists, by definition, of psychic contents which are repressed in civilization, since they contain contents that are incompatible with the attitude of consciousness. Warm and kind, Arab women are equally at ease with rage. They develop the skills to fight and attack. These women are dedicated to the protection of themselves and their loved ones, at all costs, and by all means.

The dream endows Dorit with compensatory psychic energies symbolized by the Arab women. "Wild, untamed" femininity, founded upon inherent instincts, complements Dorit's well-behaved persona and weak impersonal ego. The Arab women, an energy repressed in Dorit's unconscious, are in the service of maintaining life.

The dream's locale, Safed, is a small town nestled high in the northern Galilee mountains where Jewish mysticism evolved. An inspiring vessel, Safed is the birthplace of the Zohar, the Book of Splendor, a principal Kabbalistic treatise. In contrast to Orthodox Judaism, with its strict adherence to collective masculine spirituality, Jewish mysticism emphasizes the value of individual relatedness and the Creator. Furthermore, Jewish mysticism contributes spirituality suffused with feminine elements.

The symbol "liberation of Safed" represents a psychic movement, a progression, a major shift from a collective Orthodox Judaism, a rigid, impersonal structure, toward an alternative framework. A later development than Orthodox Judaism, Jewish philosophical-theological mystical conceptions embrace and incorporate femininity. Safed's mystical contributions symbolize a favorable psychic balance between the masculine and feminine within the monotheistic worldview.

Dorit's dream depicts her struggle for individuation. A psychic shift, reflected in the symbol "liberation of Safed," represents the need to turn away from collective masculine Logos laws and turn toward the spiritual femininity imbued by Eros. Eros is the psychological function of relatedness which thrives when spirit and instinct are in harmony. The path to freedom, the capacity to weave feminine elements into the masculine framework via mysticism, is a process of psychic transformation filled with dangers, symbolized in the dream by Dorit's individual encounter with professional snipers. To move toward a different religiosity which emphasizes an inner unique path, based on "spiritualized femininity," requires Dorit to face heroic tasks. No wonder she is terrified to be all on her own, to become a heroine.

Dorit is provided a way not to be naively and recklessly heroic but, through the Arab women's energy, to maintain caution in the face of a transpersonal religious task. The monotheistic feminine ego is weakened and lacks the Goddess' innate instinctual sacred power. This power is miraculously transmitted to Dorit by the Arab women, mediators of the ancient female powers of the Goddess.

In contrast to the Massadah dream, which portrayed a diagnosis of a psychological state where the monotheistic spirit emasculated its femininity, the Safed dream is prognostic. Its prognosis is the heralding of the potential for imbuing spirituality with feminine elements. An inner battle is to be waged within modern-day feminine psyches in order to attain a balance between masculine and feminine energies. Fraught with doubts and conflicts, the individuation symbolized by the snipers in Dorit's dream is lonely and frightening.

A religious dream deals with transpersonal psychic contents, hence its sacredness and numinosity. The numinosity of Dorit's dream brings healing. These healing qualities are reflected by the archetypal "nodding of the head," a sign to be given by the Arab women according to the dream image. A prominent feature in the Greek Aesculapian healing temples, the nodding of the God's head in dreams was the yearned for *numen*, awaited by the sick to indicate that their prayers were answered through divine intervention. The historical numen signaled a resolution of conflicts, a state of healing. This dream's numen motif may carry a promise of healing, the mending of monotheistic split and repression of feminine contents, symbolized by the victory of the army in liberating Safed. Safed religiosity endowed the feminine with renewed honoring and reunited the traditional masculine spirit with "spiritualized femininity."

Massadah and Safed Dreams

THE Hebrew monotheistic religion, as any other religious faith, consists of the articulation of belief systems. These belief systems always parallel the psychological state of the religious followers, their ego development, their degree of consciousness. When the human ego evolves, transformations take place in the religious belief system. The Massadah and Safed dreams are both symbolic representations of Hebrew monotheistic stages in ego development.

Sara's "Massadah Dream" depicts an early phase in the Hebrew monotheistic ego consciousness. Strict collective adherence to rigid masculine dogma characterized the initial patriarchal orthodoxy. At this early stage, God, the archetype of the Self, the transpersonal supreme values, was perceived to demand strict observance to the Torah-Pentateuch articulation of His masculine logos laws. The Hebrew word תּוֹרָה = Torah means "the instruction of the right path." This developmental level of Hebrew ego consciousness was dominated by God's *tremendum* (awesome aspects), "the fear of God is the beginning of wisdom" (Psalms 110:1).

New spiritual transcendent values were one-sided, neglectful of opposite earthly-instinctual psychic contents. Psychic balance was absent. The danger of one-sidedness is reflected in the Massadah dream, the historical location where collective suicide, in the name of loyalty to spiritually transcendent values, took place.

Dorit's "Safed Dream," on the other hand, portrays the struggle for personal liberation from collective dogma, and has taken place many centuries later. Ego consciousness has evolved and allowed for expansion and flexibility. Psychic balance was restored as feminine eros elements were added to the early masculine beliefs, through the mystical beliefs of the Kabbalah. Safed was a place where the Kabbalah began: many early writings come from Safed. The Hebrew word קַבָּלָה = Kabbalah connotes a feminine attitude of "receiving." Now God, the archetype of the Self's supreme transpersonal values, has become suffused with *fascinosum*, numinous aspects of love and grace. A warm loving relationship between human and God is supported, allowing a direct dialogue, conceived of individual differences. Ultimately, this evolution of ego consciousness reflects a greater spiritual faith in God.

Active Imagination:
An Autonomous Rejection by the Unconscious— A Dialogue Between a Modern Feminine Ego and an Arab Woman

---

> *The highest and most decisive experience of all [is] to be alone with [one's] own self, or whatever one chooses to call the objectivity of the psyche. The patient must be alone if he is to find what it is that supports him when he can no longer support himself. Only this experience can give him an indestructible foundation.*[1]

THE Goddess' female earthly energies were long forsaken in Western civilization, exiled and repressed in the unconscious collective psyche, despised and denigrated. By now these ancient feminine psychic contents have become autonomous complexes in the unconscious. Complexes are defined as autonomous groups of emotions and ideas constellated around particular archetypes, accompanied by strong affects. Could it be that present-day conceptions concerning the conscious integration of ancient feminine contents, a voluntary endeavor executed by modern-day women's egos, are met with unconscious resistance and objection by such complexes? Is there an objection by the complexes to be conscious-

---

[1] C. G. Jung, *Collected Works*, vol 12, ¶32.

ly integrated? Engaged in the analytical process, analyst and women analysands aspire to reconnect with the Goddess' transpersonal earthly energies by bringing up to consciousness this material, split-off from the ego for millennia. What if these attempts fail, due to independent resistance of the complexes to be integrated in modern-day feminine consciousness?

These reflections were elicited as Norma, a young New York actress, brought in an active imagination, a dialogue between herself and an Arab woman, a psychic product of her unconscious. Active imagination is a Jungian method of self-expression that assimilates unconscious contents in order to establish communication between consciousness and the unconscious.

Norma identified her ego with the archetypal image of an innocent, defenseless, shadowless "good little girl" and was hoping that the dialogue might yield these very psychic contents, repressed within her, which she yearned to reunite with through conscious integration. Norma elected to conduct the dialogue with an opposite female energy, personified by an Arab woman who embodied a "complementary" archetypal image of grounded earthly energies. Norma anticipated being reconnected to her split-off mature womanhood. In her words, "I wish to learn how to become skilled at courageous self-defense and self-protection."

Norma had never met an Arab woman, but they seemed to her to be appropriate to carry her projections for all that her ego lacked. Arab women embodied, thus, compensatory psychic contents. Agents of the Goddess, they relied on an innate, instinctual resourcefulness. Norma projected an absolute confidence, the capacity to carry oneself with dignity through life's misfortunes, onto the Arab woman.

Norma brought much of the complex of the "good little girl" to the actual active imagination. Rather than dialoguing calmly, with some objectivity, she felt needy and emotionally starved. Slipping fast into the tight grip of her sense of worthlessness, she stressed her deprivation. She clung to the Arab woman, conveying her intense need to be sheltered, her compulsive desire to lean, moreover, to be mothered. Perhaps this inner dynamic influenced the efficacy of her communication with the Arab woman, thus curbing the conscious introjection of her unconscious product.

Thus she asked the Arab woman to take her on and teach her. The Arab woman responded in a surprising, lengthy soliloquy:

"I live in a stark naked desert. You, my dear, are too fragile to persevere through the daily hardships over there. The only thing you know how to do is to go to school, and you cry a lot.

"The reality of the place is harsh. The open horizon, the starry nights, the blue sky, they all lie. The truth is the fierce heat during the day, the sharp winds blowing sand continually in your face, the scarcity of water. Without an outer protection in the desert and without skills at enduring these hardships, there is no room for you."

Pausing for a moment, the Arab woman continued: "For me you will be an additional burden. My only intent is my own survival. No, my dear child, I have no interest in taking you or teaching you."

Norma did not succeed in dialoguing further. She was shocked that her offer to join the Arab woman in her natural habitat was refused.

The Arab woman's response to Norma raises an objective dilemma which transcends Norma's individual psyche, including her particular ego fragility during the active imagination. Could Norma's single "active imagination" hint at an objective impersonal state? Is it valid to hypothesize that the attempts by the feminine ego to reunite with its severed unconscious contents are resisted by unconscious complexes? Could then autonomous complexes of female primeval energy represented by the Arab woman negate integration by contemporary consciousness?

What makes modern women analysands assume that they will be embraced by transpersonal feminine contents buried in their unconscious? Why do they expect to relate smoothly to a value carrier of the Goddess' power, as represented by Norma's internal image of an Arab woman, without trials and tribulations? Are there some rituals to be reinstated? Is there no need for a period of apprenticeship? Maybe a candidacy phase is called for? Perhaps today's women must prove themselves fit for the task of reconnection to these transpersonal archetypal Goddess powers?

I believe that Norma's active imagination deserves serious contemplation.

CHAPTER FIVE

Erotic-Sensuous Femininity—
The Exiled Terrain of Sacred
Passion

Dream: A Holy Communion

—◦◦◦—

What is behind all the desirousness? A thirst for the eternal.[1]

> *Look, The Day of the bed*
> *The Day the Lord exalts the woman*
> *The Day she gives life to her lord*
> *she gives the harvest power to her lord*
>
> . . .
>
> *She wants it*
> *she wants the bed*
> *she wants it*
> *the joy of her heart bed*
> *she wants the bed. . .*[2]

The ritual of the hieros gamos *is religious. Through the power of instinct within her . . . a woman gains a new relation to herself. The power of instinct within her is recognized as belonging not to herself, but to the non-human realm, to the goddess . . . her sexuality, her instinct, are expression of a divine life force.*[3]

---

[1] Heraclitus in John Burnet, *Early Greek Philosophy* (London: 1892), p. 141.
[2] "Look the Day of the Bed," a poem for the Sacred Marriage Ritual, written about 2500 B.C., Mesopotamia. Rendition by Betty Meador, *Uncursing the Dark* (Wilmette, IL: Chiron, 1992), p. 62. Used by kind permission.
[3] M. Esther Harding. *Women's Mysteries* (New York: Harper & Row, 1976), pp. 151ff.

ANITA, a music teacher in analysis, brought the following dream to the analytical session. In her words, it is midnight in a small Oriental town, teeming with life even at this late hour and suffused with an air of intrigue and mystery.

I am lying with my lover on a bed near a window which overlooks a narrow, winding alley. Across the way, on the other side of the alley, is a big plaza, the town square. Although I am almost carried away by passion, surrendering to Love, I become aware of a fascinating activity. As I look through the window, I notice a large gathering of people in the town square. An extraordinary spectacle unfolds before my eyes. A sacred dance is taking place in the utter stillness of the night. Women, dancing with graceful steps, move steadily around and around in a circle. They move in complete silence, their colorful costumes and rich attire a testimony to their various countries of origin. They had traveled far to participate in and celebrate a communal feast, perhaps worshipping a common Deity, I think, as I gaze with awe at what seems to be a holy ritual, a universal religious ceremony enacted at midnight.

"It must be a Goddess, a feminine deity, that all these women worship," I speculate, and then return my full attention to my lover. The sensual pleasures I experience are now compounded by a sublime elation. Now I am not only passionately engaged but also surrounded by an unknown, yet trustworthy sisterhood. Together these two events create what I would term, for lack of a better term, "a spiritual passion."

I pondered Anita's definition, "spiritual passion." How succinct! This term will be put to good use by me. I asked Anita for the context as well as any associations regarding the dream. Anita commented: "The dream took place while I was on a Christian retreat. I was frustrated being there, listening to tiresome discourses on an abstract Spirit. Too much presence of our pious male God was disappointing. These lengthy theological discussions led me nowhere. The elements of the dream were totally alien," Anita explained. She could contribute no personal associations to the dream's images. "The Oriental town, the religious midnight worship, even the uninhibited sexual encounter are not part of my familiar reality. Perhaps the dream consists of archetypal symbols, but they seem foreign, unrelated to my conscious attitudes." She admitted being intrigued by the dream's enchanting contents, yet she could not supply relevant amplifications. Mystified, Anita nevertheless concluded that the dream had cryptic qualities. "I am so sorry that I am not capable of decoding these cryptic images."

This virginal big dream was left untended. I understood Anita's dream to emerge as an *enantiodromia*, an appearance from the unconscious of opposite contents in relation to the experience of the Christian retreat. When an extreme one-sided tendency dominates conscious attitudes, an entantiodromian counterposition breaks through to consciousness in order to balance psychically the prevailing extremity. The retreat's verbal sterility was compensated by complementary elements, bestowed by the archaic Goddess. The sacred vulva of the female deity expressed itself, replenishing a contemporary feminine psyche with "spiritual passion."

Anita's dream reflects a reawakening in a modern-day woman's psyche of feminine ancient archetypal representations.

This constellation of contents is symbolized by images surrounding the Love Goddess. In the Love Goddess' cosmogony, erotic-sensual energies were reconciled with reverent religiosity. Surrendering to sensual-sexual desires was seen as a devotional path, a religious channel to worshipping the Love Goddess.

A "passionate spirituality," to use Anita's term, incorporates erotic-sensuality and religiosity. This coexistence, which characterize the Love Goddess, appointed Her archetypal image in charge of human passions. The Goddess sanctified human passion.

In Anita's dream the synthesis of sacredness with erotic-sensuality occurs in accordance with the Love Goddess' cosmogony through the simultaneous lovemaking as the female devotees practice the sacred ritual. Though at this time it still appears in an unconscious form, a dream, the contemporary feminine is committed to the redemption of the erotic soul.

Three dreams of my women analysands are quoted in this context in view of their thematic juxtaposition of erotic-sensuality with notions of holiness. Theresa, a physician raised in a strict Catholic family, brought the following dream.

> *Four proselytizers approached my childhood home. They knocked at our door. However, instead of dispensing Holy Books, they dispensed "sex education" texts. I was startled not see the expected, conventional religious material. I thought to myself "sexuality is becoming a holy subject." Later, I was amazed to observe these illuminating books, truly eye-openers.*

Irena, a librarian, elevated her dream lover with religious numinosity. A repressed woman, she narrated her dream, shocked at its intensity.

I make love with a man. Suddenly he is transformed into Christ. Our lovemaking is superhumanly blissful.

Irena commented how much more alive she felt after this dream and how her psychic reality, usually filled with shame and guilt, seemed hopeful and optimistic.

Mira, an introverted artist, told of her recent dream in one of our sessions.

It is a sacred female ritual. Our entire group is naked and we paint erotic symbols on each other's bodies. Surprised at myself, I add a "third-eye" symbol, thinking that maybe I need to change the inferiority I feel about my sexuality. The third-eye symbol links sensuality and holiness in many cultures.

Mira's dream reflected an attempt, still unconscious, to reconcile the archetypal split between the "whore" and the "sacred priestess."

Spontaneous reunification, a sanctified union, which emerged in my analysands' dreams, reveals the mysteries of sacred sensuality, manifesting once more its vitality in the human soul. In the dream, renewed acknowledgment is given by the autonomous collective psyche to the eternal view of interconnectedness, manifested through ritualistic "passionate spirituality." Unknowingly, in the dream, Mira personified the sacred priestess, holding anew the tension between erotic-sensuality and religious devotional psychic energies.

A quest for the reunion with the ancient, split-off, psychic energies of the Love Goddess and Her votary, the sacred priestess expressed in the dream states, within the modern feminine unconscious acquires a religious status, since it mirrors a redemptive opus of the erotic psyche. The process of consciously assimilating these feminine transpersonal contents for each woman analysand takes a long time. Assimilation is accomplished very slowly, as each analysand discovers her individual destiny.

> *If a religious attitude returns to the earth, the woman will regain her self-respect. The way of a woman in the understanding of herself and the instinctual ways of the world, this is also the meaning of religion. The way of her loving comes from her inner core. Her sexuality . . . is love . . . is prayer . . . is spirituality.*[4]

---

[4]Dunn Manuela Mascetti, *The Song of Eve* (New York: Fireside/Simon & Schuster, 1990), p. 42.

The Harlot:
An Ancient Goddess and Her Agents—
The Sacred Priestess and the Ordinary Prostitute

There is no consciousness without discrimination of opposites.[5]

The tendency to separate the opposites . . . is absolutely necessary for clarity of consciousness . . .[6]

If we conceive the opposition to be sexuality versus spirituality, then the mediatory content born out of the unconscious provides a welcome . . . for the spiritual thesis . . . and also the sexual antithesis.[7]

She is sitting by the window, combing her hair
In your eyes she is a Harlot
And in my eyes she is Pure
My heart is so bitter today.
Since She is no more, my Soul is gone . . .[8]

---

[5]C. G. Jung, *Collected Works*, vol. 9.I, ¶178.
[6]C. G. Jung, *Collected Works*, vol. 14, ¶470.
[7]C. G. Jung, *Collected Works*, vol. 6, ¶825.
[8]Chaim Nachman Bialik, "She is Sitting by the Window," in *The Collected Poems* (Tel Aviv: Dvir, 1997), p. 295. Translation mine.

TRANSPERSONAL earthly feminine erotic-sensuality had been in the past the divine carrier of soul passions. Passionate desires and yearnings, contained in the erotic-sensual vessel permeated the Goddess of the ancient universe, who was portrayed by the archetypal image of the harlot. Inanna of Sumer and Ishtar of Babylon were called "The Harlots of Heaven."

In Bialik's poem, the first line, "She is sitting by the window, combing her hair," reflects a spontaneous emergence of the archetypal "harlot" in the window. An ancient ivory wall carving depicts the Babylonian Goddess Ishtar seated in a window. This position of Ishtar was termed *kilili musrint*.[9] It connotes "kilili who leans out," and demonstrates the archetypal harlot. Within the context of the cosmogony of the early Goddesses, Innana and Ishtar, erotic-sensual femininity was represented by the archetypal image of the harlot. One of the principle personalities of the Babylonian Goddess Ishtar was "Har—Mother of the Harlots." Ishtar's priestess was the *Harrie*, a spiritual ruler of the city of Ishtar. Ishtar says of herself "A Prostitute compassionate am I."[10]

The ancient harlot represents a neutral symbol, free and unencumbered by stigma or moral evaluations. No marked distinction is as yet made between sacred and profane. Both aspects of the harlot demarcated service to the Goddess.

Bialik elevates the harlot's archetypal image into a drama. His poem expresses a contemporary judgment by the collective

---

[9]According to Anne Baring and Jules Cashford in *The Myth of the Goddess* (London: Penguin, 1991), "The ancient texts also give an image of a Sumero-Akkadian goddess, Kilili, a name shared by Inanna and Ishtar. Inanna and Ishtar were both called Kilili." See pp. 216, 510.

[10]Nor Hall, *The Moon and the Virgin* (New York: HarperCollins, 1980), p. 11 and Barbara Walker, *The Women's Encyclopedia of Myths and Secrets* (San Francisco: HarperSanFrancisco, 1982), p. 820.

in regard to the harlot archetype: "In your (plural) eyes she is a harlot." Bialik sees the psychic context of the collective consciousness as biased, polluted by the historical struggle waged on the Goddess' ancient universe via the new faith in a masculine "Heavenly" God.

Bialik's poem succinctly conveys a predicament created by the monotheistic ideology that split the harlots into opposite polarities and vehemently rejected them both.

The poet retains the positive soul value of the harlot "sitting by the window, combing her hair" as a pure, precious, inspiring image. She is his muse, vital for his creative expression, and the poet declares that her disappearance implies a personal catastrophe, no less than an extinction of his soul. For Bialik, she is a vital inner figure, his own "innocent feminine side," a regenerative anima. Furthermore, she is perceived by Bialik as his daimon, a Greek Platonic conception of one's personal guardian angel. Above all, she personifies the sacred priestess aspect of the harlot.

Nonetheless, the poet's individual voice in no way represents a shared consensus with the "greater collective." Through the monotheistic centuries, she personifies the ordinary prostitute aspect of the archetypal harlot which, in the eyes of the collective, is a derogatory entity. The primordial harlot's archetypal image is no longer perceived as having redeeming qualities.

It is psychologically fascinating to note that the term פְּרוּצָה = prutza = harlot, used by Bialik, is a term currently loaded with moral indignation. It nevertheless owes its innermost meaning to its etymological root PRZ, which connotes life's flow. Thus, פְּרוּצָה = prutza = harlot is connected via the Hebrew root to פֶּרֶץ = peretz = a breakthrough, הִתְפָּרְצוּת = hitpartzut = an eruption, excitement, outburst. Thus, "harlotry" means a breakthrough into the sacred realm of the divine. "Prutza" retains the harlot's primeval connotation, that of the affirmation of life. In this way, the Hebrew patriarchal language conveys, unknowingly, the Goddess' precious cosmogony. Significantly, the biblical פֶּרֶץ = *peretz* is a hero destined to be, genealogically, an early predecessor to the Holy "Dynasty of King David," of which Christ is a direct descendant. Thus words seem to carry potency of their own, the potency of "breaking through."

The two opposing poles of the harlot's archetypal image are the sacred priestess and the ordinary prostitute. Even though clearly distinguished from each other, they belonged to the same archetype. An archetype is ultimately indivisible. Its contrary manifestations are fueled by an identical source of psychic energy. Ultimately, the opposites are one and the same.

While psychic opposites are an inevitability, inherent in the experience of any archetype, they need not be perceived as hostile rivals. The sacred priestess and the ordinary prostitute shared a common denominator, a profound sense of service to the Goddess. The sacred priestess and the ordinary prostitute represented complementary channels of erotic-sensual powers. Through their respective personifications, an embodiment of a religious vocation, as contrasted with an ordinary profession, they were both servants of the harlot, bound by mutual sisterhood, each vital in Her modality, each balancing the other.

The Goddess' concomitant duality was brought to my analytical work through an analysand's dream. Amy, an artist, shared her dream. She was still filled with awe.

> *I enter a cave. Except for the dim flickering of a fire, a remnant in the corner, I am enveloped in darkness. In the middle of the cave I notice a female figure. Gradually I can see her better, and realize that she is*

not a regular mortal. She reminds me of a Paleolithic Venus which seems ordinary in my dream state. The most striking feature about this Venus' appearance is a rapid alternation of her skin color, switching quickly between black and white. The two colors soon do not matter any more. I have a deep knowledge that I am in this cave for a remarkable event. The "woman = Goddess" greets me with a blessing. I am startled to notice that I am completely naked. I remain calm and composed when She approaches and paints my whole body with incomprehensible signs. I guess these are ritualistic symbols. I experience erotic sensations as she proceeds to paint all over.

Amy was in the fourth year of analysis. She described the dream's "numinous sense of otherness" and further observed: "The dark cave reflects an encounter with the dark recesses of my unconscious. In the cave I am initiated into feminine mysteries, a compensation to my rational masculine ego orientation. The Venus figure embodies the ancient Love Goddess, hence the emphasis on any erotic-sensual awakening.

"I believe that the most significant message of my dream consists of the image of the Goddess' oppositional nature. She is interchangeably black and white, alluding to the psychological reality of the Love Goddess. I learn that She is realized by her opposite representations, her value carriers, in an equal manner. I associate the white to the sacred priestess and the black to the prostitute according to traditional "pure" versus "shadowy" collective perceptions. I must further explore my dual initiation."

Amy ended the session enthralled with an autonomous psychic life that provides her with clear individual guidance. She commented: "Our entire work seems often like a lesson that has no boundaries, a truly obscure maze. For once, I am being given detailed direction, to explore the Love Goddess within the context of her opposite manifestations."

What is the significance of understanding the opposites for the development of the psyche? Theoretically, the conscious holding of the opposites is teleological. Its purpose is to create a tension. Holding to both opposites in consciousness is of major importance. A conflict between the opposites occurs within a difficult process, which is to be finally resolved by the discovery of a new attitude—and its adoption. An emotionally unbearable tension precedes changes and renewals. Thus, the impediment, the adversity is paradoxically a potential for psychological transformation and personality growth. New attitudes are created only through conflictual adversity of the contrary opponents. An ego expansion takes place through the conscious assimilation of hitherto repressed opposite contents.

The contraposition of any archetypal representation is arranged, generally, through a contrariety between the attitude of the conscious mind and the opposite tendency, repressed in the unconscious. Some degree of tension between consciousness and the unconscious is unavoidable and psychologically necessary.

> [T]he tendency to separate the opposites . . . is absolutely necessary for clarity of consciousness . . . when the separation is carried so far that the complementary opposite is lost sight of, and the blackness of the whiteness . . . is no longer seen, the result is one-sidedness, which is then compensated from the unconscious without our

---

[11]C. G. Jung, *Collected Works*, vol. 14, ¶470.

help. The counterbalancing [can] bring about a
catastrophic *enantiodromia*.[11]

Therefore, repressed contents must be made conscious.
Optimally the ego is not to be possessed by either opposite.

When it comes to shedding light on the innate opposites of
the early Love Goddess, the sacred priestess and the prostitute,
the general laws of opposition do not apply. Little is known
about the historical sacred priestess, and the prostitute is burdened with negative projections of the split-off transpersonal
erotic-sensual energies. A carrier of inhuman *tremendum numinosum*, the prostitute is burdened with an "unholy" burden that
has little in common with her innate nature. What went wrong?
Why is our knowledge of the sacred Goddess minimal, skewed,
and distorted?

About 10,000 years ago, a new god emerged in human consciousness. Historically, an enormous transformation in consciousness took place, the result of continual developmental
processes and ongoing autonomous shifts in the human psyche.
A fierce struggle ensued, in regard to sovereignty, between the
primordial feminine Goddess and the new faith in the masculine God.[12] New tenets were introduced: the spirit, ego consciousness, ethical concepts, logos' laws. This change caused an
irreconcilable dichotomy between the old and new orders. A
cosmic battle was waged against the previous cosmogony of a
feminine Earth Goddess. The rise of monotheism, faith in a masculine, heavenly God, belongs ultimately in the realm of theology. It concerns a numinous conflict directed at a discovery of
an appropriate notion of Self (Wholeness = Holiness), as incar-

---

[12]Phyllis Boswell Moore, *No Other Gods* (Wilmette, IL: Chiron, 1992), p. 183.

nated by an appropriate archetypal image of the Supreme Deity. Psychic energies were mobilized in monotheism and recruited to the service of the cosmic struggle between the deities' cosmogonies. The Goddess had to be defeated.

What was the price for this cosmic revolution in terms of an inner discrimination between the harlot's two opposite personifications? Matters were not contained within the Goddess' opposition any more. The conflict was no longer inner-directed, focused on a differentiation between the sacred priestess and the prostitute. A complete *enantiodromia* to the previous, primordial worldview brought about an opposition between the deities. All efforts were harnessed toward a different, greater opposition: the cosmic struggle between feminine and masculine worldviews, redefined by now as "flesh/spirit," "profane/sacred" dichotomies. The latter acquired broader meanings.

Under the new ideology, the natural polarities within the harlot archetypal image, the sacred priestess and the ordinary prostitute, were neglected and forgotten. Erotic-sensual feminine passion sank into an unconscious repression. The harlot archetypal image, a feminine ancient Goddess, was reduced in its entirety by collective Judeo-Christian morality. It was considered an exclusively negative, lowly, and inferior matrix, devoid of spirituality. The Goddess represented by the harlot archetypal image was identified solely with the prostitute polarity. The denial of the Goddess' divinity brought about an annihilation of the sacred priestess polarity.

Psychologically, the entire realm of human passions lost its connection to the sacred with the rise of monotheism and the oppression of the Goddess. Threatened by extinction, the brittle new faith in a masculine God abolished erotic-sensual passions. The feminine realm was curtailed; its vitality was forbidden.

Desecrated from then on, split off from their sacred core, erotic-sensual energies were identified by the new religion as "unholy." Exiled into unconsciousness, little knowledge about the sacred priestess remained. The denigrated "flesh," the wretched female body symbolized by the prostitute, was doomed to a condition of hopeless inferiority. As stated before, the prostitute polarity has been inflated by projections of archetypal transpersonal layers that assumed *tremendum numinosum* properties. The prostitute polarity became an evil seductress, bewitching, endowed with shadowy attributes.

The psychological battle waged by believers in the masculine Supreme Deity desecrated the archetypal image of the Goddess. Hostilities against feminine erotic-sensual powers have left the harlot image soulless, Her divinity denied. The extinction of religious attributes given to feminine erotic-sensual energies within the original sacred matrix brought an end to the role of the sacred priestess. Passions were no longer honored as providing spiritual nutrients to the psyche. The sacred priestess has been forsaken ever since; her memory has been erased within monotheistic consciousness.

When feminine sacredness is denied, and spiritual mysteries banned, the human psyche suffers violation. Not only is it greatly impoverished, it is imprisoned in soullessness. Both men and women suffer.

The Sacred Priestess:
Votary of the Goddess' Divinity—
Psychopomp, Mentor, Mediator

Help us to return to You
Renew our days as in the past.[13]

Sexuality is not mere instinctuality; it is an indispensable creative power that is not only the basic cause of our individual lives, but a very serious factor in our psychic life as well.[14]

Sexuality is the strongest symbol at the disposal of the Psyche.[15]

IN THE early days, transpersonal erotic-sensuous energies belonged in the domain of a female deity. In an interconnected universe, the ancient Goddess was a symbolic archetypal representation identified with the unfathomable mystery of nature and its own ultimate cyclical nature. Her cosmogony conveys the vision of Oneness, an ecstatic apotheosis to nature's sanctified unity, an indivisibility which surrounds all. The Goddess' theogeny conceived of the interrelated-

---

[13]A Hebrew prayer, paraphrased.
[14]C. G. Jung, *Collected Works*, vol. 8, ¶107.
[15]C. G. Jung, transmitted by Dr. Elinor Bertine.

ness of sensuality and spirituality. Sexuality was viewed as one of epiphanies of earthly life, a basic divine law of life.

Sensuality and spirituality converge in a holy communion. The bestowing powers of transformative erotic-sensual energies were believed to be the Goddess' channels, in her capacity as Love Goddess, commanding spiritual ecstasy and sensual delights. The pleasures of sexual abandonment were inspired by the Goddess and were assessed as "the nearest experience to bliss." It was assumed that sexuality was not to be owned by humans. Rather, people offered themselves to the generative powers of the Goddess through sensuality-sexuality. Human sexuality was an expression of Her divinity, serving as a rekindling of the Sacred Spark of Life. Sexual passions were perceived as physical manifestations of spiritual devotion to the Goddess—a form of worship. The Love Goddess was venerated by her initiates. The word *venerate* originates in the Latin words *venerari,* connoting an attitude of reverent worship, and *veneris,* which connotes love, sexual desire. Venus' name (the Roman Love Goddess) is derived from *veneris.*[16]

It is sometimes asserted that in ancient times people were more open to spirituality because they lived closer to the deities. Psychologically, this assertion connotes that they had an immediate access to the transpersonal objective psyche. Ancient wisdom conveyed keen observations about the human soul.

Ancient languages are instructive in their profound understanding of human psychology, the "logic of the unconscious," as implied by their etymology. Words, seemingly unrelated in their meanings, are connected by an identical root. Looked at closely, these connections to an identical root provide deep insight con-

---

[16]Nancy Qualls-Corbett, *The Sacred Prostitute* (Toronto: Inner City Books, 1988), p. 118.

cerning psychological, rather than linguistic, interrelatedness. Thus, an inner, psychic linkage expressed through root commonality substantiates the etymological relatedness.

The trilateral root system of the Hebrew language (each root consisting of three letters) carries sacred meaning. Mantra-like, it is believed to exert psychic power according to various mystical Jewish traditions. The Hebrew language, even though patriarchal, reputed for "fathering" the Holy Scriptures, reveals an intimate affinity with the Goddess' cosmogony. A proximity to erotic-sensual female passions is manifested by an etymological root connection between the word "יֵצֶר = yetzer = instinct" and the seemingly unrelated "יְצִירָה = yetzira = creativity." Both instinctuality and creativity were hallowed within the Goddess' unified matrix. Instinctual vitality is a prerequisite for creative expression. The poet Rainer Maria Rilke wrote the following in his *Letters to a Young Poet*.

> Artistic creation lies so incredibly close to sex, its pain and its ecstasy, that the two manifestations are indeed but different forms of one and the same yearning.[17]

The Goddess' understanding of earthly life as consisting of nurturing elements, influences a Hebrew root commonality between "זוֹנָה = zona = harlot" and "מָזוֹן = mazon = food." Thus, the prostitute does not carry a stigma in Hebrew. Rather, she is conceived as providing essential nutrient sustenance, an elementary requirement for the smooth flow of life. "אָדָם =

---

[17]Rainer Maria Rilke, *Letters to a Young Poet* (New York: W. W. Norton, 1934), pp. 30–31.

Adam = a person" is connected by root to "אֲדָמָה = *adamah* = earth," an etymological connection close to the Goddess' cosmogony. "רַחֲמִים = *rachamim*—compassion" is tied by root to "רֶחֶם= *rechem* = uterus," a physical female locale for genuine humanness. Finally, an etymological connection is to be found between the "קְדֵשָׁה = *kedesha* = sacred priestess" and root identity with states of "קְדֻשָׁה = *kedusha* = holiness, divinity" or "קָדוֹשׁ = *kadosh* = a saint." An aspect of the Goddess' archetypal image as a harlot, the sacred priestess is perceived in the Hebrew language by her proximity to sacredness. By no means does this juxtaposition represent a patriarchal ideology. Rather, it is an apt expression, portraying the religiosity of the role of the sacred priestess, an integral part of the Love Goddess' sacred worldview.

It is not possible for humans to relate directly to transcendent numinosity. Deities cannot be integrated consciously by humans by way of an unmediated exposure. The human ego is invariably overwhelmed by transpersonal psychic contents and endangered by a state of archetypal possession. Numinosity requires mitigation, a mediation by a psychopomp, a psychic personification mediating unconscious contents to consciousness. For that reason the Goddess' erotic-sensual transpersonal passions were conveyed to humans through Her votary, the sacred priestess. Mediating was her role as a bridge between the superhuman and human. A mortal herself, the sacred priestess channeled the Goddess' essential lessons. Soul passions were constellated in the Goddess' temple through the sacred priestess' mentorship. Her modeling enabled conscious integration of erotic-sensual radiant sacredness.

A consecrated servant, spiritually receptive to feminine powers, the sacred priestess introjected the Goddess' erotic-sensual powers. Celebrating spiritual ecstasy attained through sensual delights, the Goddess' essence, Love, was realized in the sacred priestess. The sacred priestess initiated humans into the mysteries of love through her unbound erotic-sensuality.

The sacred priestess' unfettered movements conveyed in the dancing ritual mediated the dynamic transformative aspects of the Goddess' erotic-sensual energies. Paradoxically, the sacred priestess inhabited a mortal and finite body. The Goddess' immortal and infinite qualities were reflected through the sacred priestess. The mysteries of Her religious teaching, the gifts bestowed by Her, were mediated by the sacred priestess' passionate supplications.

An etymological inquiry clarifies the religious connotations of the sacred priestess. The Goddess embodied Nature. Nature is "divine," "holy," which implies "to not be touched."

The priestesses of Ishtar in Sumer (c. 3000 B.C.) were personifications of service to the Goddess and to transpersonal feminine contents. Their name was Quadishi, meaning "not to be touched"; their role transcended prostitution. The root for *Hierodule*, the Greek name for the Sacred Priestess, is *hieros*, which connotes "sacred" while *eis* means "passion."

Thus, "untouchable," "sacred" mirrored the fact that sexual engagement was not compulsory; rather, it was voluntary. The Sumerian Goddess Inanna was called "A Sacred Priestess of Heaven" as well as "A Hierodule of Heaven." The two expressions portrayed the ancient Goddess in her harlot archetypal image. The priestess and the prostitute are opposites as all archetypes are.

In later generations, under monotheistic indoctrination, the sacred priestess was reduced to the sacred prostitute. Wrestling with an acceptance of a sacred priestess = harlot = healer is a challenge for contemporary women. The "healing-holiness" connection, involving a religious attitude, is still alien. A numinous religious perspective is attained when the archetypal idea of prostitute = healer is assimilated consciously. A carrier of erotic-sensual spirituality, the sacred priestess continues to exist, buried in the Western unconscious. Her traces are rediscovered anew, as exhibited by the following dreams brought by women analysands. Their contents were redeemed to consciousness as these dreams were worked through in the analytical setting.

Barbara, a young psychologist in New York City, had the following dream.

> *I meet with my supervisor, an honorable older psychiatrist whom I highly respect. I am wearing a miniskirt which looks sleazy to me. I am indeed shocked when my supervisor tells me, "You are a true healer!" I find it hard to believe because of the way I am dressed, but he really means what he says.*

In the dream Barbara embodies the healing powers of the sacred priestess. The dream is a compensatory one since Barbara finds it impossible to combine erotic-sensuality with her earnest professional demeanor.

Sherry, a computer programmer, shared the following dream.

> *I see myself in a Temple. The priestess is veiled. Her name is Astarte [Sherry claimed not to have ever heard this name]. I am following a nun walking with her donkey as she goes on her way to the desert. I tell her: "I want to learn about celibacy." I throw a veil over her donkey. Instead of the customary white veil I am startled to find myself throwing a scarlet veil.*

Sherry, a devout Catholic, did not find a celibate nun in her dream. Instead, the spontaneous features of the sacred priestess emerged: the red veil symbolizes feminine erotic-sensuality.

Martha, a social worker in New England, brought an initial dream to our analytical work.

> In my dream you are a beautician. Your task is to teach me about appropriate make-up. Stunned, I commented: What a vain, superficial task my dream assigns to you.

When Martha associated to the details of the make-up, I amplified on the spiritual dimension of facial adornment in ancient civilizations. Actually, the facial design in Martha's dream resembled the ancient Egyptian facial design necessary for entering eternal life, as instructed in *The Egyptian Book of the Dead*. So I, the analyst, was entrusted with the sacred priestess' tasks as a "spiritual beautician."

The loss of sacred femininity to contemporary consciousness is psychologically very significant. An absence of holiness implies an estrangement from transpersonal feminine psychic layers. The feminine's essential meaning to the human psyche is reduced when the sacredness of the vulva is unacknowledged and denied.

One aspect of feminine transpersonal psychic energies, erotic-sensual desires, is an integral part of spiritual femininity. Vehemently persecuted for two millennia, erotic-sensual feminine energies, personified by the ancient sacred priestess in the Goddess' temple, are no longer known. It seems, however, that a rehabilitation of erotic-sensual powers in their spiritual dimensions may be heralded in the present through the conscious integration of the ancient attitudes toward erotic-sensual sacredness as embodied by the sacred priestess, the Goddess' human votary.

An elucidation of the sacred priestess can be a partial answer to the missing values in contemporary feminine psyches. Rescuing the sacred priestess from the remote recesses of the collective unconscious is a *via regia* to the redemption of the feminine erotic soul. I believe that re-remembering, and the re-collecting of the sacred priestess' archetypal essence provides one with the true psychological meanings, its numinous essence. The enormous resurgence of feminine contents from their lengthy exile in the collective unconscious is by now agreed upon. This movement, which I call "The Return of the Feminine Principle," has been directed autonomously by the objective psyche. Its *teleos* is a furthering of the development of human consciousness. The historical shifts involve present-day women, profoundly affecting them in all spheres of their personal lives. A conscious relatedness to the "Goddess' sacred vulva" symbol seems a constructive route, although a most complex one, since the Goddess' as well as the sacred priestess' archetypal images are erased from our memory and little documentation is to be found about them. Their conscious rediscovery provides an empowering pathway to restore feminine wholeness (= holiness) which includes new (or remembered) feelings of dignity and self-worth.

Can the Feminine Erotic Soul be Redeemed by Modern Women?

━━◆━━

I am falling fast down. Falling fast. Falling, falling, I realize that I cannot stop the rapid descent nor control its rapid pace. I am terrified. Suddenly, Big Hands support me from beneath, containing me securely. The Big Hands belong to a non-human feminine figure, perhaps a Goddess. Upon waking I hear a whisper: "You have arrived Home."[18]

*Come with me on the night journey of my soul
Please bring forth love and light to transform the blackness into gold.*[19]

I AM often asked the following questions: "What is the key to relate to the remote past?" "By what mode are we to integrate the ancient psychic contents?" Individuals familiar with C. G. Jung's writings, ask me, "How can we translate the belief-systems and practices of past feminine *Weltanschauung* ("worldview," "philosophy" in German) and incorporate them in our present-day reality in the Western world?" "In what way can modern-day women connect to the

---

[18]An initial dream brought to the first session by Cecily, a weaver.
[19]Aurora Terrenus, unpublished poem. Used by kind permission.

Goddess' sacred priestess and Her erotic-sensual energies?"
Finally, an ultimate question-exclamation is heard: "What do we
do about redeeming the feminine erotic soul?"

An experienced analyst learns to anticipate a familiar
response, an inseparable question-exclamation by the analysand,
when discussing a serious predicament: "But what do I do about
it?" This human response often coincides, or even precedes, the
verbal formulation of the analysand's dilemma, before adversity
can "sink in," before a clear grasping of her plight has been
attained.

Silence and patience are ill-afforded in times of transition. As
tension, anxiety, even panic, mount, "doing something about it,"
an extroverted attitude which seeks resolution and relief by
deeds, is what we are accustomed to in our Western civilization.

My response to the obstacles involved in the conscious integration by modern women of the material discussed in this manuscript is a cautious one. I have given serious thought to these
questions but I cannot provide practical answers. It is not my
role, I humbly acknowledge.

As a Jungian analyst, I endeavor to remain loyal to inner
guidelines. The historical shift that I call "the return to the feminine principle" from its exile in the collective unconscious for
two millennia, has been acknowledged in the Western world.
The origins of this enormous transpersonal event, on such a
scale, cannot be planned by mortals. Rather, this event, determined autonomously by the objective psyche, is directed at an
evolution and development of human consciousness. The resurgence to consciousness of feminine psychic contents must pro-
duce theoretical conceptualizations, an intellectual body of ideas,
even a consistent system of beliefs, in regard to its manifestations.
In numinous times, such as the return of the feminine principle

to collective consciousness, ideological and political viewpoints are necessary byproducts.

Prophets and pioneers are possessed by definition. Seized by psychological states of identification with numinous transpersonal contents which herald historical changes, they are caught in the grip of a superhuman transcendence. Yet, to be harshly analytical of the ardent feminist ideology to which many women agreed several decades ago is not the answer. Indeed, the early feminists expressed the concerns of many. The ideological political movement had profound merits. It intensified the bond between and among women; it served as a reminder of powerful women's gatherings held in the past to celebrate and honor the feminine. Above all, it constellated hopes for change! It provided an article of faith, by way of a teleological-purposeful manifesto, which beckoned toward a desired future path.

However convincing it might be, any ideology, even if necessary and of great service, is involved in one-sided tendencies. A responsible psychological attitude involves the challenge of holding the opposites in consciousness. An enthusiastic identification with an ideological viewpoint means a dangerous possession by archetypal contents. Such are the inherent pitfalls of the political arena, which are humanly unavoidable when emotions seize us in their grip. The transpersonal requires a state of grace. One cannot forcefully enter a sacred temenos by will power alone. Ideology is insufficient in the realm of the numinous. Pioneers cannot bend and force life's plans by sheer determination.

Central to the present discourse is the lack of conscious honor granted by the early feminists toward the holiness of erotic-sensual feminine psychic aspects and the absence of the ancient sacredness of the Goddess' vulva, a seat of feminine self-worth and dignity. A reconciliation of religious spirituality with erotic-sensual femininity was alien to early feminist ideology. The absence of this reconciliation between spirituality and sensuality has created further obstacles for contemporary women who seek consciously to realize an opus such as the redemption of the feminine erotic soul.

Contemporary women no longer seem to be their father's daughters, protected from their own passionate erotic-sensual nature by an oppressive monotheistic legacy. Their introjected masculine values prevent their true liberation. An encounter with their inner sacred priestess' erotic-sensuality, split off and alive, living in the unconscious of every woman, is simply terrifying.

"What? Me?" cry out alarmed analysands when erotic-sensual imagery appears in their dreams. Monotheistic axioms solidly incorporated by modern women combine with a long tradition of denials, suppression, and inhibition when erotic-sensual energies are concerned. Holding tight to her cultivated persona, each projects erotic-sensuality to an inferior shadowy domain, ruled by prostitutes and pornography. In Greek, *porne* means "a harlot," and "pornography" connotes writing about harlotry. Psychologically, it is the archetypal image of the harlot, an ancient divinity, that is behind the projections. For this reason the split-off realm of unfettered lust and sheer voluptuousness constellates numinosity. Numinosity is experienced whenever transpersonal archetypal psychic layers are inwardly touched. When fear and dread are at the base of this experience, the numinous assumes negative qualities, termed *tremendum numinosum*. A communal "resistance" to the integration of the sacred erotic-sensual powers of past feminine sovereignty is founded in powerful psychic factors that determine modern women's psychological reality.

At the root of this predicament is great loss. The loss of ancient feminine sacredness is also a severance from the Goddess' sacred vulva. The spiritual dimension of the feminine matrix, its transpersonal divinity, cannot be related to consciously. These psychic contents have been severed from feminine development for too long. A conscious reconnection to feminine sacredness is a vital prerequisite to an authentic feminine development. Psychologically, as long as feminine sacredness is repressed, women are not able to rely on their inner self-esteem. Since the establishment of monotheism, masculine structure has retained its holiness, its connection to a male deity. Women are ungrounded as long as they claim equality with the masculine, for conscious reconnection to their feminine holiness is absent.

Feminine transpersonal archetypal psychic layers are represented symbolically by an image of the Goddess' sacred vulva. An objective and autonomous timeliness is required to mend the split between modern women and their split-off sacredness. Healing woundedness requires a transformative process that cannot be rushed, in accordance with the proverb coined by ancestral wisdom: "To everything there is a season, and a time to every purpose" (Ecclesiastes 3:1).

There is a need to rediscover age-old containers within which feminine sacredness is celebrated. Based on archetypal transpersonal patterns, all women participated in periods of solitude; for example, the monthly acknowledgment of menstrual cycles. Women's mysteries originated in the intimate proximity of the feminine to Nature, and through bodily changes. The feminine as a collective has to reinstate these traditional vessels, to consciously reexperience transpersonal visitation as conception, pregnancy, childbirth, and lactation.

My experience as a Jungian analyst has taught me to honor psychic resistances. One defense mechanism, termed "resistance," reflects a psychological state (or place) where fears and anxieties must be defended against. Such a psychological place merits an attitude of patience and compassion from the analyst. One predicament of modern-day women is their profound resistance to reconnecting to their own erotic-sensual powers, repressed in the unconscious psyche. Their difficulties in consciously honoring the sacredness of their erotic-sensual powers is well-respected and understood by me.

My training has handed me the appropriate tools to relate to psychic contents: the development of a symbolic attitude in seeking the meaning behind our inner and outer lives. The symbolic attitude is a viable mode for modern women, for it is of great service in attaining a conscious relatedness to archetypal transpersonal layers, the locale where ancient feminine sacredness is to be explored and discovered. Basic concepts underlie the symbolic approach. The collective unconscious, or the objective psyche, is composed of archetypal patterns. Archetypes function autonomously in universal unchangable patterns. These "pure" eternal forms are filled with human experiences. Human experiences provide the changing contents. Based on historical times and geographical locales, empirical contents vary, thus archetypes provide containers for daily experiences throughout the various civilizations. An archetype cannot be related to directly. Only their imagined representations, or symbols, are accessible to consciousness.

The unconscious is expressed by symbols. Jung understood the symbol as the "best possible representation of something that can never be fully known."[20] While archetypes exist eternally,

---

[20]See *Symbol*, glossary.

they manifest in reality as symbols. Paradoxically, the symbol is a bridge. Although anchored in daily experience, the symbol points to an archetypal eternity, enabling our limited understanding to touch a transcendent unknowable reality. Earnest awareness of archetypal symbols renders the unconscious as conscious as is humanly possible.

Perhaps, then, an answer to the central question, "What is the key to relate to the remote past?" is to be found in the development of a symbolic attitude. Understanding symbols requires modern women to acquire access to the language of the unconscious, a capacity to connect consciously to the feminine ancient matrix, to the Goddess' sacred vulva, to the sacred priestess, and to feminine erotic-sensuality.

Contemporary women may choose an individual path via the analytic process, in order to establish conscious relatedness to their personal unconscious images. Others may elect to participate in group gatherings in celebrating, through rituals, the honoring of their femininity. Inner or outer, introverted or extraverted choices, all provide an opportunity to apply symbolic consciousness.

Recently I received a letter from Lora, who had been an analysand of mine over a decade ago, when she was a young student in New England. Lora is a bright young woman, gifted in many areas. She contributed to my endeavor, of which she is aware, by permitting me to quote her letter verbatim:

> *Dr. Hillel, last week I thought of you a lot as I was preparing to give a belly-dance performance in C, Maryland. First of all, C is in the middle of redneck nowheresville, USA. The performance was held in an American Legion Hall, normally a bastion for men*

and male energy. There I found myself in a large basement room with a number of other female performers, all of us preparing for our respective dances. The women participating were of all sizes, shapes, and ages, predominantly older. Many of them were none too traditionally beautiful. Stage makeup is much darker and heavier than normal makeup, and under normal lighting it makes women look like whores.

So there I was, slightly nervous before my performance, in a dark basement full of whorish looking women. Part of me was horrified—asking myself what in the world I was doing there, had I indeed taken the wrong exit off the beltway? Yet, another part of me remained calm, knowing that the women were all there in homage to their deepest and most sensual femininity, whatever form that took for each one. And, indeed, in costumes, under the lights, all the women, no matter if they were physically beautiful or not, looked very feminine and not at all like cheap whores.

It occurred to me that by belly dancing, these women, myself included, were all sacred priestesses devoted to the Goddess, heeding an inner call to the worship of the feminine.

After the performance, which ended very late, I found myself to be strangely and simply rejuvenated. At the same time I felt very contented at knowing that through this belly-dance evening I had connected to a deep level of my feminine being.

I realized that I had embodied the Goddess in a modern-day circumstance. The ancient and the modern *joined together this one evening, opening the door to the feminine eternal.*

I share with you my own personal experience of this female contact with the divinity. If you have the opportunity, try some belly dancing and see if you, too, have a similar experience!

What I like best about Lora's letter is her suggestion that I try belly dancing. Indeed, I think I may.

The Reality of the Psyche

A Premonitory Dream

For thou wilt light my candle . . .
will enlighten my darkness.

—(PSALMS 18:28)

SOME time ago, while working on
an article in a library, I was exploring Jungian themes on the subject of "psychic reality and its manifestations." This inquiry
evoked crucial questions which, at the time, seemed unanswerable. That night I had a dream. Was it dreamed in response to my
questions, awakened during the day, while sitting in the library?
The dream went like this:

I live on an island, a remote location in the midst of a
lush tropical setting. Each room in the beach hotel I am
staying in offers an exquisite view onto the magnificent
ocean which envelopes the island, isolating me from
familiar environs, from my past. As I walk to my room,
through a dimly lit long corridor, I notice on the floor
a pile of books, covered by thick layers of dust and spi-
der webs. Here are treasures of the human mind,
shoved aside, forlorn in the midst of primeval nature.
"Primordial," "untamed," "untouched," are this far-off

island's features. No accepted norms of civilization or culture are to be discerned in this uncouth locale. Instead, there is an unlimited splendor, provided by Nature—landscapes and seascapes of magnificent beauty.

The collection of books found in the corridor contains the works that would be part of a well-endowed library. The book collection seems bizarre, moreover, absurd, within the context of the island's alien, blissful ignorance. Among the books, I discover an old edition of "Jung's Writings," attached to "A Guide to the Island's Mysteries." It seems an odd volume, combining two independent subjects. The volume is bound in brown leather upon which gold letters are printed. Immediately upon seeing this book, I am resolved to have it, keenly aware that no one around here is ever going to notice that this book is missing.

A year later, I found myself spending several months in Hawaii. At the time of the dream, my conscious ego had absolutely no pre-knowledge of my future visit.

In Hawaii I began to write about the Goddess as a symbol of earthly sensuality. Within the lush tropical setting, surrounded by an ocean, I wrestled with a study of feminine erotic-sensual aspects within a Jungian perspective, in accordance with my dream's directive. The dream was realized, incarnated in a concrete mode. Even though not as primitive as the dream's scape, the Hawaiian reality replicated the dream's essence. My dream's "Guide to the Island's Mysteries" disclosed that the atmosphere characteristic to the islands, my inner island and Hawaii, were closely connected to female sensuousness.

This synchronicity demonstrates one of Jung's basic tenets in regard to the reality of the psyche. Governed by different laws, the psyche is infinite by definition. It transcends the limitations of time and space, and is not bound by past or future parameters. Hence, the psyche's autonomous premonitory qualities which are revealed by dreams.

Hawaii provided an excellent container for my efforts. Beyond the wild profusion of colors and scents, deeper female sensuous energies lie dormant. The magnificence of the land is a manifestation of a voluptuous Goddess' splendor, waiting to be discovered and consciously explored.

Glossary of Jungian Terms[1]

—◆—

Active Imagination: A method of assimilating unconscious contents (dreams, fantasies, etc.) through some form of self-expression.

Anima (Latin "soul"): The unconscious, feminine side of a man's personality. She is personified in dreams by images of women ranging from prostitute and seductress to spiritual guide (Wisdom). She is the eros principle, hence a man's anima development is reflected in how he relates to women. Identification with the anima can appear as moodiness, effeminacy, and over-sensitivity. Jung calls the anima "the archetype of life itself."★

Animus (Latin "spirit"): The unconscious, masculine side of a woman's personality. He personifies the logos principle. Identification with the animus can cause a woman to become rigid, opinionated, and argumentative. More positively, he is the inner man who acts as a bridge between the woman's ego and her own creative resources in the unconscious.★

Archetypes: Irrepresentable in themselves, but their effects appear in consciousness as the archetypal images and ideas. These are universal patterns or motifs which come from the col-

---

[1]Entries with an asterisk are from Daryl Sharp, *C. G. Jung Lexicon: A Primer of Terms and Concepts* (Toronto: Inner City Books, 1991). All other entries are from the standard glossary compiled by Daryl Sharp and used in Inner City Books' publications. Used by permission.

lective unconscious and are the basic content of religions, mythologies, legends, and fairytales. They emerge in individuals through dreams and visions.★

Association: A spontaneous flow of interconnected thoughts and images around a specific idea, determined by unconscious connections.★

Collective Unconscious: A structured layer of human psyche, containing inherited elements, distinct from the personal unconscious.

Compensation: A natural process aimed at establishing or maintaining balance within the psyche.

Complex: An emotionally charged group of ideas or images. At the "center" of a complex is an archetype or archetypal image.★

Constellate: Whenever there is a strong emotional reaction to a person or a situation, a complex has been constellated (activated).★

Ego: The central complex in the field of consciousness. A strong ego can relate objectively to activated contents of the unconscious (i.e., other complexes), rather than identifying with them, which appears as a state of possession.★

Enantiodromia: A Heraclitan term which captures constant change. Literally, it means "running counter to," and refers to the emergence of archetypal changes demanded by the evolving unconscious opposite in the course of time. Whenever an aspect of the archetypal totality is unrecognized in consciousness, it generates a change factor in the psyche.

Feeling: One of the four psychic functions. It is a rational function which evaluates the worth of relationships and situations. Feeling must be distinguished from emotion, which is due to an activated complex.★

Hieros gamos: Sacred marriage; *mysterium coniunctionis*; the mystery of the union of opposites.

Individuation: The conscious realization of one's unique psychological reality, including both strengths and limitations. It leads to the experience of the Self as the regulating center of the psyche.★ In addition: A teleological purposeful principle and process, informed by the archetypical ideal of psychic wholeness, which underlies all psychic activities. Its goal is the development of the individual personality.

Inflation: A state in which one has an unrealistically high or low (negative inflation) sense of identity. It indicates a regression of consciousness into unconsciousness, which typically happens when the ego takes too many unconscious contents upon itself and loses the faculty of discrimination.★

Introjection: A process of assimilation.

Intuition: One of the four psychic functions. It is the irrational function which tells us the possibilities inherent in the present. In contrast to sensation (the function which perceives immediate reality through the physical senses) intuition perceives via the unconscious, e.g., flashes of insight of unknown origin.★

Libido: "Libido for me means psychic energy, which is equivalent to the intensity with which psychic contents are charged" (CW7, p. 52, note 6).

Logos: Psychologically, a capacity for judgment, insight, discrimination, differentiation; a masculine psychic function.

Participation mystique: A term derived from the anthropologist Lévy-Bruhl, denoting a primitive, psychological connection with objects, or between persons, resulting in a strong unconscious bond.★

Persona (Latin "actor's mask"): One's social role, derived from the expectations of society and early training. A strong ego relates to the outside world through a flexible persona; identification with a specific persona (doctor, scholar, artist, etc.) inhibits psychological development.★

Prima Materia: An alchemical term meaning "original matter." Psychologically, raw material.

Projection: The process whereby an unconscious quality or characteristic of one's own is perceived and reacted to in an outer object or person. Projection of the anima or animus onto a real woman or man is experienced as falling in love. Frustrated expectations indicate the need to withdraw projections, in order to relate to the reality of other people.★

Psychic Energy: Libido.

Psychopomp: A psychic factor that mediates unconscious contents to consciousness, often personified.

Puer aeternus (Latin "eternal youth"): Indicates a certain type of man who remains too long in adolescent psychology, generally associated with a strong unconscious attachment to the mother (actual or symbolic). Positive traits are spontaneity and openness to change. His female counterpart is the *puella,* an "eternal girl" with a corresponding attachment to the father-world.★

Quaternity: An image of fourfold structure. Psychologically, it points to the idea of wholeness.

Religious Attitude: Psychologically, an attitude informed by the observation, and respect, for invisible forces and personal experiences. "Religion designates the attitude peculiar to consciousness which has been changed by experience of the *numinosum*" (CW 11, ¶9).

Repression: The unconscious suppression of psychic contents that are incompatible with the attitude of consciousness.

Self: The archetype of wholeness and the regulating center of the personality. It is experienced as a transpersonal power which transcends the ego, e.g., God.★

Senex (Latin "Old man"): Associated with attitudes that come with advancing age. Negatively, this can mean cynicism, rigidity, and extreme conservatism; positive traits are responsibility, orderliness, and self-discipline. A well-balanced personality functions appropriately within the *puer-senex* polarity.★

Shadow: An unconscious part of the personality characterized by traits and attitudes, whether negative or positive, which the conscious ego tends to reject or ignore. It is personified in dreams by persons of the same sex as the dreamer. Consciously assimilating one's shadow usually results in an increase of energy.★

Symbol: The best possible expression for something essentially unknown. Symbolic thinking is non-linear, right-brain oriented; it is complementary to logical, linear, left-brain thinking.★

Synchronicity: A phenomenon where an event in the outside world coincides meaningfully with a psychological state of mind.

Temenos: Greek word meaning "a sacred protected space."

Transcendent function: The reconciling "third" which emerges from the unconscious (in the form of a symbol or a new attitude) after the conflicting opposites have been consciously differentiated, and the tension between them held.★

Transference and countertransference: Particular cases of projection, commonly used to describe the unconscious, emotional bonds that arise between two persons in an analytic or therapeutic relationship.*

Transformation: A process experienced as a renewal or rebirth of the personality.

Uroboros: The mythical snake or dragon that eats its own tail. It is a symbol both for individuation as a self-contained, circular process, and for narcissistic self-absorption.*

Bibliography

Apocrypha of the Old Testament. London & New York: Thomas Nelson and Sons, 1957.

Baring, Anne and Jules Cashford. *The Myth of the Goddess.* London: Penguin, 1991.

Beauvoir, S. de. *The Second Sex.* New York: Alfred Knopf, 1953.

Bialik, Chaim Nachman. *Collected Poems.* Tel Aviv: Dvir Publications, 1997.

Bible. *The Holy Bible.* Authorized King James Version. Oxford: Oxford University Press, n.d.

Bolen, Jean Shinoda. *Goddesses in Everywoman.* New York: HarperCollins, 1984.

Burnet, John. *Early Greek Philosophy.* London, 1892.

Cavafy, C. P. *The Complete Poems of Cavafy.* Orlando: Harcourt Brace, 1984.

Christ, C.P. *Diving Deep and Surfacing: Women Writers on Spiritual Quest.* Boston: Beacon Press, 2nd ed., 1986.

———. *Laughter of Aphrodite: Reflection of a Journey to the Goddess.* San Francisco: HarperSanFrancisco, 1988.

Claremont de Castillo, Irene. *Knowing Woman: A Feminine Psychology.* New York: Putnam's Sons, 1973.

Downing, C. *The Goddess: Mythological Representation of the Feminine.* New York: Common Press, 1984.

Douglas, Claire. *The Woman in the Mirror: Analytical Psychology & the Feminine.* Boston: Sigo Press, 1990.

Eliade, Mircea. *A History of Religious Ideas.* Chicago: University of Chicago Press, 1983.

Gimbutas, Marija. *The Language of the Goddess.* New York: HarperCollins, 1989.

Goldenberg, N. *Changing of the Gods: Feminism and the End of Traditional Religion.* New York: Crossroad, 1984.

Hall, Nor. *The Moon and the Virgin.* New York: HarperCollins, 1980.

Harding, M. Esther. *The Way of all Women.* New York: Harper Colophon, 1975.

———. *Women's Mysteries: Ancient and Modern.* New York: Harper & Row, 1976.

Hopke, Robert. *A Guided Tour to the Collected Works of C. G. Jung.* Boston: Shambhala, 1982.

Jung, C. G. *The Archetypes and the Collective Unconscious*, vol. 9.I of *The Collected Works*, Bollingen Series XX. R. F. C. Hull, trans. Princeton: Princeton University Press, 1959.

———. *Civilization in Transition,* vol. 10 of *The Collected Works,* Bollingen Series XX. R. F. C. Hull, trans. Princeton: Princeton University Press, 1964, 1970.

———. *Memories, Dreams, Reflections.* Aniela Jaffé, ed. New York: Pantheon, 1961.

———. *Mysterium Coniunctionis*, vol. 14 of *The Collected Works*, Bollingen Series XX, R. F. C. Hull, trans. Princeton: Princeton University Press, 1963.

———. *Psychological Types*, vol. 6 of *The Collected Works*, Bollingen Series XX, R. F. C. Hull and H. G. Baynes, trans. Princeton: Princeton University Press, 1971.

———. *Psychology and Alchemy,* vol. 12 of *The Collected Works*, Bollingen Series XX, R. F. C. Hull, trans. Princeton: Princeton University Press, 1953, 1968.

————. *Psychology and Religion: East and West,* vol. 11 of *The Collected Works,* Bollingen Series XX, R. F. C. Hull, trans. Princeton: Princeton University Press, 1958, 1963.

————. *Two Essays on Analytical Psychology,* vol. 7 of *The Collected Works,* Bollingen Series XX, R. F. C. Hull, trans. Princeton: Princeton University Press, 1953.

————. *The Structure and Dynamics of the Psyche,* vol. 8 of *The Collected Works,* Bollingen Series XX, R. F. C. Hull, trans. Princeton: Princeton University Press, 1960.

Kramer, Samuel N. *From the Poetry of Sumer.* Berkeley: University of California Press, 1979.

————. *The Sacred Marriage Rite: Aspects of Faith, Myth, and Ritual in Ancient Sumeria.* Bloomington, IN: Indiana University Press, 1969.

Mascetti, Manuela Dunn. *The Song of Eve* (New York: Fireside/Simon & Schuster, 1990.

Meador, Betty. *Uncursing the Dark.* Wilmette, IL: Chiron, 1992.

Moore, Phyllis Boswell. *No Other Gods.* Wilmette, IL: Chiron, 1992.

Mylonas, G. *Eleusis and Eleusinian Mysteries.* Princeton: Princeton University Press, 1961.

Neumann, Erich. *The Great Mother: An Analysis of the Archetype.* Ralph Manheim, trans. Bollingen Series XLVII. Princeton: Princeton University Press, 1955.

Olson, C. (ed.). *The Book of the Goddess, Past and Present.* New York: Crossroad, 1983.

Paris, Ginette. *Pagan Meditations.* Dallas: Spring, 1986.

Patai, Raphael. *The Hebrew Goddess.* New York: KTAV, 1967.

Perera, Sylvia Brinton. *Descent to the Goddess: A Way of Initiation for Women.* Toronto: Inner City Books, 1981.

Qualls-Corbett, Nancy. *The Sacred Prostitute.* Toronto: Inner City Books, 1988.

Reed, E. *Women's Evolution: From Matriarchal Family.* New York: Pathfinder Press, 1975.

Rilke, Rainer Maria. *Letters to a Young Poet.* New York: W. W. Norton, 1934.

Sharp, Daryl. *C. G. Jung Lexicon: A Primer of Terms and Concepts.* Toronto: Inner City Books, 1991.

Terrenus, Aurora. *The Shroud of Sophia.* Santa Cruz, CA: Celestial, 1988.

———. *Sophia of the Bible.* Santa Cruz, CA: Celestial, 1988.

Ulanov, Anne Bedford. *The Feminine in Jungian Psychology and in Christian Theology.* Evanston, IL: Northwestern University Press, 1971.

Wagner, Richard. *Tannhäuser in Full Score.* New York: Dover, 1984.

Walker, Barbara. *The Women's Encyclopedia of Myths and Secrets.* San Francisco: HarperSanFrancisco, 1982.

Whitmont, Edward C. *Return of the Goddess.* New York: Crossroad, 1982.

Wolkstein, Diane and Samuel N. Kramer. *Inanna: Queen of Heaven & Earth.* New York: HarperCollins, 1983.

Woodman, Marion. *Addiction to Perfection.* Toronto: Inner City Books, 1982.

———. *The Owl Was a Baker's Daughter.* Toronto: Inner City Books, 1980.

———. *The Pregnant Virgin.* Toronto: Inner City Books, 1985.

Index

A

active imagination, 93
alchemical solution, 13
allergies, 47
ambivalence, 46
Aphrodite, 50, 51
archetypal feminine, 27
archetypes, 127

B

Baring, Anne, 28, 106
Bialik, Chaim Nachman, 105
Book of Ruth, 61, 62

C

case histories
   Amy, 108, 109
   Anita, 100
   Barbara, 119
   Betty, 74
   Cecily, 122
   Dorit, 84, 86, 87, 88, 89, 92
   Gloria, 74
   Hilary, 70, 71
   Irena, 102, 103
   Joanna, 75
   Leah, 65
   Lisa, 73
   Lora, 128
   Martha, 120
   Mira, 103
   Marianne, 68
   Miriam, 39, 40
   Nora, 15
   Norma, 94–95
   Rita, 72
   Sally, 46, 49, 73
   Sara, 79, 81, 82, 83, 91
   Sharon, 58
   Sherry, 119
   Susan, 11
   Thelma, 71
   Theresa, 102
Cashford, Jules, 28, 106
Cavafy, C. P., 67
Chagall, Marc, 46

D

dawn, 53
deliverance, 84

dream
    emergency, 12
    healing the wounded vulva,
    15
    holy communion, 99
    Jung and the vulva, 9
dreams, 11, 18, 22, 49, 50, 51,
    74, 131, 133
    big, 21, 22, 23
dreamwork, 67, 68, 70

E
ego
    modern feminine, 93
Eleusinian rituals, 70, 71
enantiodromia, 22, 40, 101, 112
Enheduanna, 53
Epiphany, 35, 36, 39
Eros, 16
erotic-sensual potency, 29
erotic-sensual feminine
    energies, 31, 46
erotic-sensuality, 14
    sacred, 72
erotic-sexuality, 73

F
fascinosum, 92
fate, 42
feminine

alienation from archetypal
    center, 64
consciousness, 14
earth-sensuality, 14
ego, 86
groundedness, 66
quandary, 7
restoration with
    monotheism, 77
return of principle, 123
sensuality, 33, 35
values, 31
femininity
    erotic-sensuous, 97
    loss of sacred, 120
flesh/spirit, 112

G
gazebo, 37
gleaning, 57
Goddess, 70, 81
    cosmogony, 27
    defeated, 29
    image of, 6, 134
    Love, 28, 102
    projecting evil on, 29
    veiled, 35
Goddesses, 13, 39
goodness, one-sided, 29

H

Harding, M. Esther, 99
harlot, 105, 107
    archetypal image, 112
    inner, 72
Heraclitus, 99
hero, tormented, 41

I

Inanna, 106
    hymn to the goddess, 36
Inanna and Ebeh, 6
inauguration into feminine
        sensuality, 33
independence, 16
instinctual-sensual matrix, 47
Ishtar, 106, 118

J/K

Jung, C. G., 21, 25, 63, 67,
        105, 110, 114
kabbalistic teaching, 30
Kiddish, 26
Kiddush-HaShem, 81
kilili musrint, 106
Kramer, S. N., 35

M

maidenhood, 86

mana, 14
Massadah, 80, 81
Massadah dream, 79, 89, 91
masculine contents
        possession by, 65
Meador, Betty, 6, 28, 36, 53,
        99
mediator, 114
mentor, 114
monotheism, 77
Moore, Phyllis Boswell, 111

N

Nature, 13, 14, 118
numen motif, 89
numinosity, 25, 125

O/P

opposites
    understanding, 110
passion
    sacred, 97, 100, 101
Passover Haggadah, 25
Perera, Sylvia B., 64
persona, 87
    loving, 74
priestess, 28
    sacred, 69, 105, 108, 112,
        114, 117, 118, 121

prima materia, 54
profane/sacred, 112
prostitute, 105, 108, 112
prostitute-healer, 119
psyche, reality of the, 131
psychic contents, 27
psychic imbalance, 12
psychopomp, 40, 114, 117
purpose of the work, 25

Q/R
Quadishi, 118
Qualls-Corbett, Nancy, 115
redemption, 23
  from Egypt, 26
resistance, 127
return to feminine roots, 54
Rilke, Rainer Maria, 116

S
Sabbath benediction, 26
sacred dimension, 25
sacredness
  denial of, 66
Safed, 85, 88
Safed dream, 84, 89, 91
  liberation of, 88
  self-fulfillment, 16
self-realization, 16
self-respect, 104

sexual engagement
  renunciation of, 82
shadow
  denial, 86
  feminine, 82
  tendencies, 74
shock, 13
sisterhood, 82
  celibate, 83
soul
  feminine erotic-122
spirit, 14
suicide, 80
  diagnosis of feminine
    collective, 79
synchronicity, 49

T
Tannhäuser, 41 ff
Tefilin, 26
Terrenus, Aurora, 25, 122
tiqqun, 30
transference-counter-
    transference, 23
transpersonal archetypal
    contents, 22
transpersonal feminine
    contents, 118
tremendum, 91
tremendum numinosum, 113

U/V

unbound from the past, 55
vagina, 13
Venus, 43
vulva
    as sacred place, 13
    goddess' sacred, 124, 126
    loss of goddess' sacred, 63
    regained sacred, 67
    sacred, 16, 66, 69, 101

Vulva Song, 10

W

Wagner, Richard, 41
Walker, Barbara, 106
woundedness, 14

Y

Yetziass Mitzraim, 25

Dr. Rachel Hillel was born in Israel, raised in a pioneering Israeli kibbutz, spent her adolescent years in Europe, and later served as an officer in the Israeli army. Because she loves music, she pursued a degree from the Tel Aviv Music Conservatory. She earned a B.A. in psychology and philosophy, an M.A. in clinical psychology, and her Ph.D. in Clinical Psychology and Philosophy from Tel Aviv University. Her Jungian training, attained from the Israel Association of Analytical Psychology, was completed in 1977. She has been in private practice since 1974. She travels a great deal, and lived for many years in the United States. She has lectured for the International Congress of Jungian Analysts, the National Conference of Jungian Analysts, the Jung Foundation in New York, the Jung Institutes in Chicago, Boston, and San Francisco, the Montreal Jung Society, the Ottawa Jung Society, and the Friends Conference for Religion and Psychology, in addition to lecturing in Australia, Mexico, New Zealand, and in her native Israel. She has five wonderful children. She is working on a second book called *My Biblical Heroines.*